Economics for a Beautiful World

Sharon Thompson

Economics for a Beautiful World

© 2022 Sharon Thompson

Published by Texianer Verlag
Johannesstraße 12
78609 Tuningen
Germany
www.texianer.com

for
The Hugh & Helene Schonfield
World Service Trust
www.schonfield.org

ISBN: 978-3-949197-94-9

This book follows the structure of *Sacred Economics* by Charles Eisenstein licensed under a Creative Commons Attribution 4.0 International License and freely available at https://sacred-economics.com/read-online/ as pdf file or in print form by North Atlantic Books (July 12, 2011) ISBN 978-1583943977 and *The Politics of God* – Hugh J. Schonfield ISBN: 9783949197895 with the permission of the Hugh & Helene Schonfield World Service Trust

ABOUT THE AUTHOR

Sharon Thompson and her husband of sixty three years, Gordon, a retired dairy farmer, are the parents of six daughters (and now six sons-in-law) who have blessed them with twenty grandchildren and fifteen great-grandchildren. Her family is her greatest love and joy. Her hope is that this book will play a role in advancing a worldwide movement that will lead to a reclaimed world of love, peace, and justice for all people everywhere.

Table of Contents

ABOUT THE AUTHOR..3

INTRODUCTION...7

PART I: THE ECONOMICS OF SEPARATION....................9

    Chapter 1: The Gift World......................................9
    Chapter 2: The Illusion of Scarcity.......................13
    Chapter 3: Money and the Mind..........................17
    Chapter 4: The Trouble with Property.................21
    Chapter 5: The Corpse of the Commons...............25
    Chapter 6: The Economics of Usury.....................29
    Chapter 7: The Crisis of Civilization....................33
    Chapter 8: The Turning of the Age......................37

PART II: THE ECONOMICS OF REUNION......................41

    Chapter 9: The Story of Value.............................41
    Chapter 10: The Law of Return...........................45
    Chapter 11: Currencies of the Commons.............49
    Chapter 12: Negative-Interest Economics...........53
    Chapter 13: Steady-State and De-growth Economics....57
    Chapter 14: The Social Dividend........................61
    Chapter 15: Local and Complementary Currency..........65
    Chapter 16: Transition to Gift Economy..............69
    Chapter 17: Summary and Roadmap..................73

PART III: LIVING THE NEW ECONOMY..........................77

    Chapter 18: Relearning Gift Culture....................77
    Chapter 19: Nonaccumulation.............................81
    Chapter 20: Right Livelihood and Sacred Investing......85
    Chapter 21: Working in the Gift..........................89
    Chapter 22: Community and the Unquantifiable..........93
    Chapter 23: A New Materialism..........................97

SUMMARY OF THE POLITICS OF GOD..........................101

PART I..107

PART II..113
    Chapter 1: Twentieth Century Man...............................113
    Chapter 2: War and Law..114
    Chapter 3: One World..116
    Chapter 4: The Brink or the Eve?.....................................117
    Chapter 5: A Time of Testing..119
    Chapter 6: The Third Phase...121
    Chapter 7: Plan in Progress..123

About The Mondcivitan Movement...127

INTRODUCTION

I spent much of my adult life trying to understand the true nature of U.S. foreign and domestic policy. In my book, *We Have a Choice: Let's Just Do It*, the conclusion I eventually arrived at can be summarized in the words of Rahul Mahajan from his book *The New Crusade: America's War on Terrorism*:

> *There can be no mistake about it – the United States is an empire, the most powerful in history... Empires are always about extraction of wealth from the provinces for the benefit of the center, without regard for the subject people. They may not benefit all social strata in the imperial nation – in fact, some of the lower classes have to fight and die to maintain the empire – but they always do benefit an elite. In most cases, the wealth is spread around, both among some broad strata of the imperial center, and among a native elite in the provinces, in both cases to help preserve political stability.*[1]

I wrote that book with the express purpose of exposing the writings of author Dr. Hugh J. Schonfield to a larger audience. I had, over a period of time, come to accept the main thesis of his book, The Politics of God[2] – that a divine plan was in progress to establish a Servant Nation that would act as the catalyst to bring peace and

---

1 Mahajan, Rahul 2002, p. 101-103, *The New Crusade: America's War on Terrorism*, Monthly Review Press, New York.
2 See the relevant section in this book.

justice to the world. The response was negligible, until I shared a copy of the book with Stephen A. Engelking who offered to publish it. Although Schonfield was instrumental in establishing the nation he had envisioned, the world was not ready for it, so the fulfillment of the plan remains to be realized.

And then, Charles Eisenstein's book *Sacred Economics* came into my life. It was the "missing link" between Schonfield's vision and the practical means of carrying it out. I fervently believe we will see—as Eisenstein describes it—"the more beautiful world our hearts tell us is possible."

PART I: THE ECONOMICS OF SEPARATION

Chapter 1: The Gift World

Because our early human ancestors viewed the earth as a sacred gift from the gods who inhabited it...

...they operated in a gift economy with gifts flowing constantly until they met a present need...

...not in a barter system to maximize their rational self-interest as depicted in most economics textbooks.

PEOPLE WITH UPLIFTED ARMS ENCIRCLING THE GLOBE:

Our early human ancestors would have viewed the earth as a sacred gift from the gods who inhabited it. Can you imagine the wonder, the gratitude, of our early ancestors as they contemplated the undeserved provenance the world gave them so freely? It is no wonder that they believed the gods not only made the world, but that they gave it to them. The first is an expression of humility, the second, of gratitude.

Sadly, later theologians twisted this realization to mean, "God gave us the world to exploit, to master, to dominate." Such an interpretation is contrary to the spirit of the original realization. Humility knows that this gift is beyond our ability to master.

Gratitude knows that we honor, or dishonor, the giver of a gift by how we use it.

FIGURE OFFERING A GIFT FROM HER PLENTY:

Our ancestors operated in a gift economy. We would expect primitive people, connected with this primal gratitude of receiving the gift of the earth from the gods, to enact it in their social and economic relationships, which they did.

We also must recognize that we have embarked on a long journey of separation from this sense of divinity and created a world in which ruthless sociopaths rise to wealth and power. Today's economic system rewards selfishness and greed, not the common good.

How did the ancient gift economies work? While gifts could be reciprocal, just as often they flowed in circles, One person gives to another who gives to another and eventually the gift gets back to the original giver. The gifts flow continuously, until they meet a real, present need. Whereas money today embodies the principle, "More for me is less for you," in a gift economy, more for you is also more for me because those who have extra, give to those who are in need.

STACK OF ECONOMICS TEXTBOOKS WITH LARGE "X" THROUGH THEM:

The conventional explanation of how money developed that one finds in economic textbooks assumes barter as a starting point. According to these texts, from the very beginning, competing individuals seek to maximize their rational self-interest.

This idealized description is not supported by anthropology. Barter was a relative rarity among hunter-gatherers and other early human societies. Economic anthropologist George Dalton has written,

> *"Barter in the strict sense of moneyless exchange, has never been a quantitatively important or dominant model of transaction in any past or present economic system about which we have hard information."*

Economists, in telling the history of money, project our modern perceptions about it backwards, and with it some deep assumptions about human nature, the self and the purpose of life: that we are discrete and separate selves competing for scarce resources to maximize our self-interest. This is simply not true.

Chapter 2: The Illusion of Scarcity

People strive for the unobtainable goal of "enough" money...

...in a world of abundance and much waste...

...while their real human needs would be met in a gift world.

FIGURE:

Humankind and their relationship to money in the twenty-first century.

THOUGHT BALLOON:

How has money become the agent of scarcity? The assumption of scarcity is one of the central axioms of economics. Obviously, poverty is not due to a lack of productive capacity. Nor is it due to a lack of willingness to help. Many people would love to feed the poor, to restore nature, and do other meaningful work but cannot because there is no money in it. Money utterly fails to connect gifts and needs. Why? Many would say it is because of greed, especially that of the elite ruling class. The paradigm of greed, however, is rife with judgment of others, and with self-judgment, as well. An indication that greed reflects the *perception* rather than the reality of scarcity is that rich people tend to be less generous than poor people.

SPEECH BALLOON:

Greed makes sense, however, in a context of scarcity. Our reigning ideology assumes it. The separate self in a universe governed by hostile or indifferent forces is always at the edge of extinction, and secure only to the extent that it can control these forces. Cast into an objective universe external to ourselves, we must compete with each other for limited resources.

FIGURE REACHES TOWARD AN UNOBTAINABLE GOAL:

Amidst abundance, even people in rich countries live in ever present anxiety, craving "financial security" to try to keep scarcity at bay. And as the anxiety of the wealthy confirms, no amount is ever "enough". It may be called greed, but in actuality, it is a response to the perception of scarcity.

WASTE DUMPSTER:

We live in a world of fundamental abundance, a world where vast quantities of food, energy, and materials go to waste. In the Global South and the Global North ghettos, people lack food, shelter, and other basic necessities and cannot afford to buy them. An enormous proportion of human activity is either superfluous or detrimental to human happiness. Consider the armaments industry and the resources consumed in war, the layout of suburbia, which makes public transportation impossible and necessitates inordinate amounts of driving, the shoddy construction and planned obsolescence of many of our manufactured goods and there are many other examples.

SYMBOL OF THE GIFT WORLD:

A sacred economy would change this. People could rid the world and themselves of all this waste and only have possessions that they truly value.

Even at our current, high rate of consumption, some forty percent of the world's industrial capacity stands idle. That figure could be greatly increased without any loss of human happiness. All that would be lost would be the pollution and the tedium of factory production. The "jobs" that are lost could be devoted to labor-intensive roles like permaculture, care for the sick and elderly, restoration of ecosystems, and all the other needs of today that go tragically unmet for lack of money.

Chapter 3: Money and the Mind

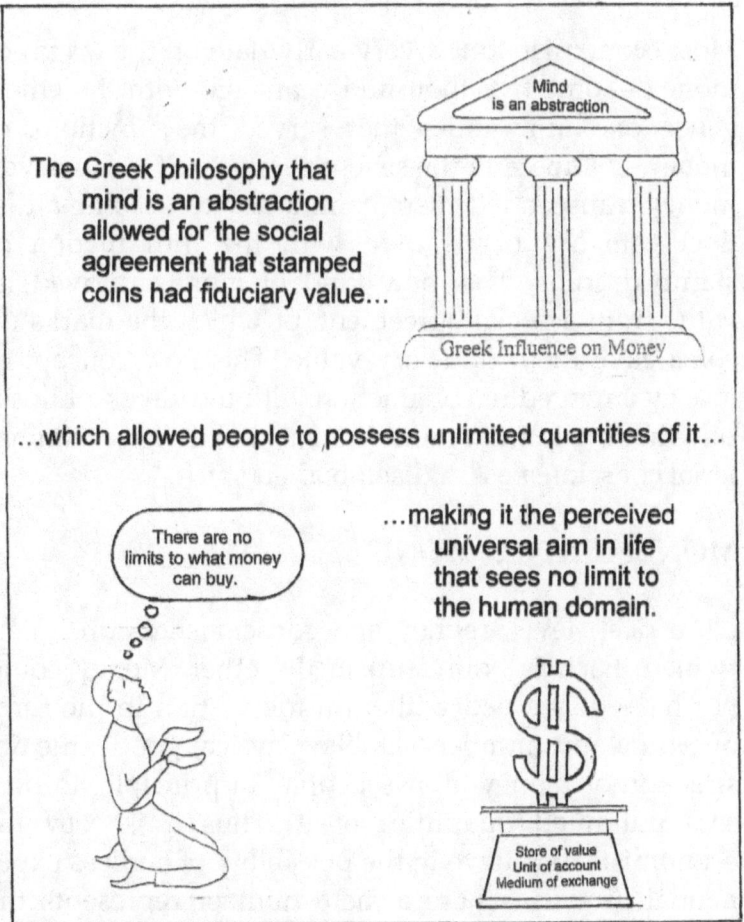

GREEK-STYLE BUILDING AND LABEL:

Most economists put a very early date on the origin of money — some five thousand years ago with the emergence of commodities that served the functions of money. In Greece in the seventh century BCE, however, money transcended mere commodity to become a distinct category of its own with the introduction of stamped coins. This new kind of money derived its value from a social agreement, of which the marks on coins gave them fiduciary value. This new concept of money emerged in conjunction with the Greek philosophy that the human mind is an abstraction — an immaterial consciousness, a disembodied spirit.

MONUMENT TO MONEY:

On a deep level, money and consciousness are intertwined. Each is bound up in the other. Money could not have developed without a foundation in the form of words and numbers. Unlike physical goods, the abstraction of money allows people, in principle, to possess unlimited quantities of it. Thus it is easy for economists to believe in the possibility of endless exponential growth, where a mere number represents the size of the economy. Lost in abstraction, economists and consumers ignore the limits of nature and culture to accommodate economic growth.

THE FUNCTIONS OF MONEY ARE LISTED ON THE MONUMENT:

While acting as a medium of exchange, money is essential and desirable. It is subject to the same limits as the goods for which it is exchanged and people's desire for it is limited by their satiety. Money as a unit of account —a standard numerical monetary unit of measurement of the market value of goods, services, and other transactions—is also essential and desirable. However, when acting as a store of value, people's desire for it can become unlimited—wealth-getting for the sake of accumulation.

FIGURE GENUFLECTING BEFORE THE MONUMENT TO MONEY:

Money is perceived to be the universal aim in life. It is a universal means as well, and indeed it is largely because it is a universal means that it is also a universal end, of which one can never have too much, or so it seems. Because there is no apparent limit to what money can buy, people's desire for money tends to be unlimited as well. We are quite accustomed to seeing money as the key to the fulfillment of all our desires. How much is enough? The reason that no amount of money can ever be enough is that people use it to fulfill needs that money cannot actually fulfill. As such it is like any other addictive substance, temporarily dulling the pain of an unmet need while leaving the need unmet. Today people use money as a substitute for connection, for excitement, for self-respect, for freedom, and for much else.

THOUGHT BALLOON OF FIGURE:

People see no limit to the human domain. They buy and sell things that they perceive as belonging to them.

Technology has widened that domain to include things like the electromagnetic spectrum and gene sequences. With no limits put on money, it is implied that the realm of the owned can grow indefinitely, to bring everything into the human domain.

Chapter 4: The Trouble with Property

How did we get from HERE...   ...to HERE?

The earth is the LORD's and the fullness thereof

PRIVATE PROPERTY NO TRESPASSING

Land ownership originated with the Roman patrician class...

...and with the passage of the Enclosure Acts in England, it became law there and throughout Europe.

Enclosure Acts

Thus, the gift of land that was given to all people was stolen and the theft encoded into law by the thieves.

PROPERTY IS THEFT

BANNER WITH INSCRIPTION:

The earth was seen by the ancients as a gift from the gods. Originally, land rights were almost always held in common, accruing to the village or tribe, and not the individual. In the great agrarian civilizations such as Egypt, Mesopotamia, and Zhou Dynasty China, there was little concept of private ownership. All land was the property of the king, and because the king was the representative of the divine on earth, all land was the property of God.

SIGN: PRIVATE PROPERTY/NO TRESPASSING:

Individuals are seen as property owners. In the United States, a property owner can restrict who can even set foot on his/her land. The situation is different in most of Europe where "trespassing" is not a concept; the land is open to all. There is mutual respect between the property owner and the person desiring the use of it.

ROMAN FIGURE:

The Roman patrician class. In the West, the absolute concept of land ownership seems to have originated in Rome. Wherever and whenever it happened, the privatization of land soon brought with it a concentration of ownership. As Rome expanded through conquest, the new lands migrated into the hands of the wealthiest families - the patrician class—setting the norm for many centuries to come. The parallel between ancient Rome and the present day is striking. Now as then, wealth is increasingly concentrated in the hands of the few. Now as then, people must go into lifelong debt that they can never pay off just to have access to the necessities of life. Then it was access to land; today it is through access to money. The slaves, serfs, and tenants gave a lifetime of labor to the enrichment of the landowners; today the proceeds of people's labor go to the owners of money.

SCROLL:

The passage of the Enclosure Acts. In England, transferring of land was generally not possible until the fifteenth century. Thereafter, the vast communal lands of England rapidly came under private ownership thanks to the Enclosure Acts, a process paralleled across the continent, for example through the "emancipation" of the serfs. Lewis Hyde writes:

Whereas before, a man could fish in any stream and hunt in any forest, now he found there were individuals who claimed to be the owners of these commons. The basis of land tenure had shifted. He [the serf] could not move freely from place to place, and yet he had inalienable rights to the piece of land to which he was attached. Now men claimed to own the land and offered to rent it out at a fee. While a serf could not be removed from his land, a tenant could be evicted not only through failure to pay the rent but merely at the whim of the landlord. As with so many social reforms, the freeing of the serfs was another step in the consolidation of economic and political power in the hands of the already powerful.

SIGN: PROPERTY IS THEFT:

The gift of land which was given to all people was stolen. If property is robbery, then a legal system dedicated to the protection of private property rights is a system that perpetuates a crime. By making property sacrosanct the law validates the original theft. This should not be too surprising if the laws were made by the thieves themselves to legitimize their ill-gotten gains. Such was indeed the case: in Rome and elsewhere, it was the rich and powerful who seized the land and made the laws.

Chapter 5: The Corpse of the Commons

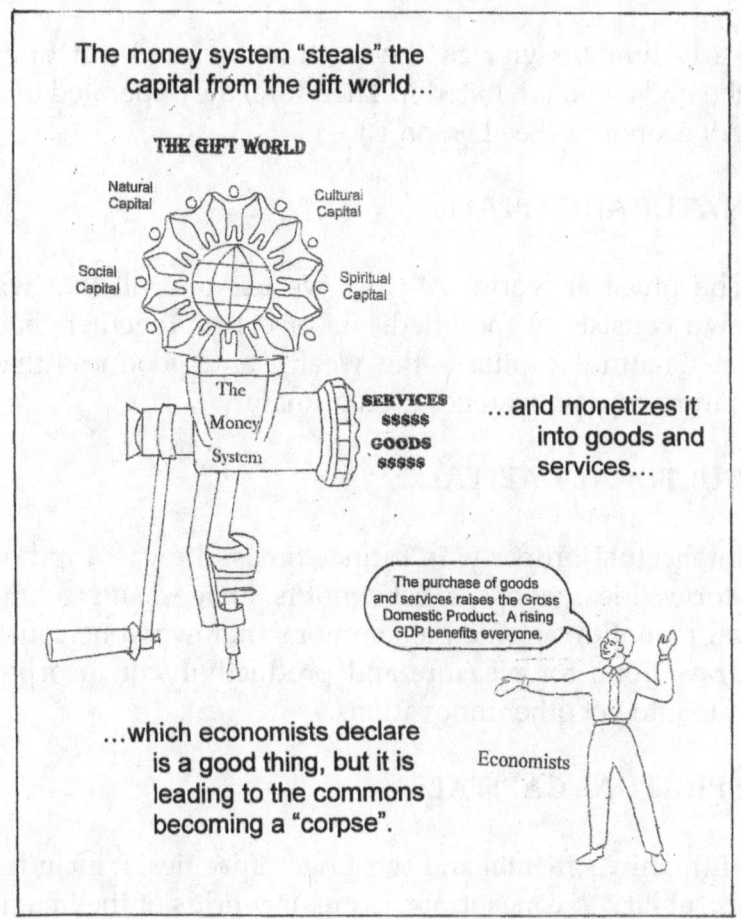

THE GIFT WORLD:

Early humans viewed the earth as a sacred gift from the gods who inhabited it. Therefore, they operated in a gift economy. (See Lesson 1.)

NATURAL CAPITAL:

The physical world. All that we use and all that we own consists of modified bits of earth. Together they are "natural capital" — the wealth and goodness that nature has bequeathed upon humanity.

CULTURAL CAPITAL:

Intellectual property. In former times, the vast fund of stories, ideas, songs, artistic motifs, images, and technical inventions formed a commons that everyone could draw upon for pleasure and productivity, or incorporate into yet other innovations.

SPIRITUAL CAPITAL:

Humanity's mental and sensuous capacities. It includes the ability to concentrate, to create worlds of the imagination, and to derive pleasure from experiencing life.

SOCIAL CAPITAL:

Relationships and skills. It includes the "services" that people once provided for themselves and each other in a gift economy, such as cooking, child care, health care, hospitality, entertainment, advice, and the growing of food, making of clothes, and building of houses.

FIGURE:

Economists. One of the two primary assumptions of economics is that human beings normally act in their rational self-interest and this self-interest corresponds to money. That is, two people will only make an exchange—buy something for money—if it benefits both to do so. Economists therefore associate money with "good". That is one reason why economic growth is the unquestioned holy grail of economic policy— when the economy grows, the world's supposed goodness level rises.

MESSAGE IN SPEECH BALLOON:

For the economy to grow, the realm of money-dominated goods and services must grow too. Money must meet more and more of humanity's needs.

Gross Domestic Product is defined as the sum total of the goods and services a nation produces. Only those exchanged for money count.

MEAT GRINDER:

The money system. A little reflection reveals that nearly every good and service available today meets needs that were once met for free in the gift world. The limited character of human needs presented problems from the very beginning of the industrial era. The solution to the looming crisis of overproduction of textiles was to manipulate people into overfulfilling their need for clothes. When one need has been generally fulfilled, it is resolved by exporting it onto some other need. So, stealing the capital from the gift world, it is monetized and then sold in the form of goods and services. The question is, what happens when all of these forms of common capital are tapped out? Humanity is witnessing the "corpse" of the commons.

Chapter 6: The Economics of Usury

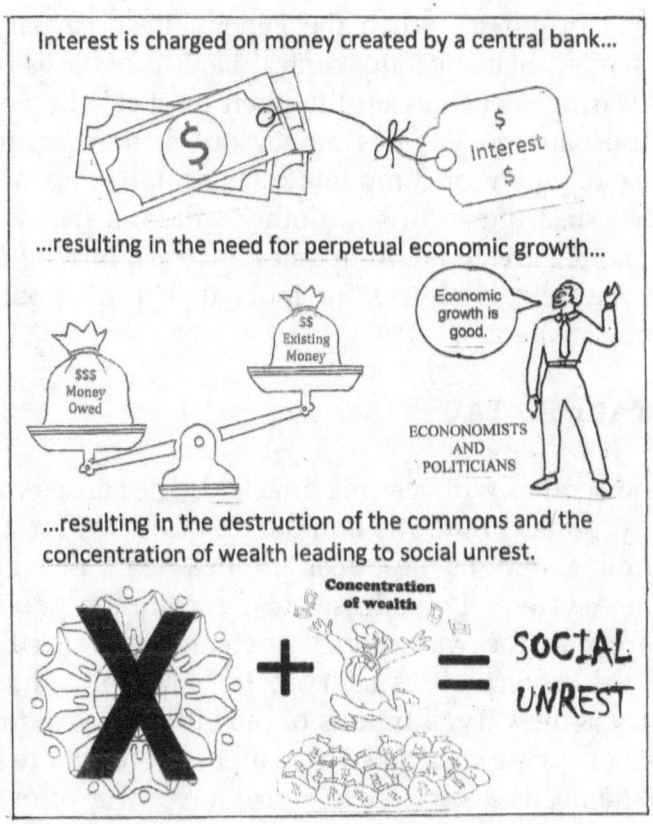

MONEY:

Money originates when the Federal Reserve Bank of the United States or any central bank purchases interest-bearing securities on the open market. The Fed or central bank creates this money out of thin air, at the stroke of a pen (or computer keyboard). It is always an interest-bearing security. In other words, it means that the money created accompanies a corresponding debt, and the debt is always for more than the amount of money created.

ATTACHED TAG:

Money comes with a string attached. The cause of insecurity, poverty, and the liquidation of our cultural and natural commons lies deep in the heart of today's money system. These losses to the common good are inherent in the way money is created and circulated and the centerpiece is usury, better known as interest. Usury is the very antithesis of the gift economy, for instead of giving to others when a person has more than he/she needs, usury seeks to use the power of ownership to gain even more—to take from others rather than to give.

BALANCE SCALE:

The imbalance between the existing money supply and the amount that is owed is due to interest. At any given time, the amount of debt exceeds the amount of money in existence To make new money to keep the whole system going, it is necessary to create more "goods and services". This is accomplished by selling something that was once free—by converting forests into timber, music into product, ideas into intellectual property, and social reciprocity into paid services.

FIGURE ON RIGHT AND SPEECH BALLOON:

The message of economists and politicians.

It is economic dogma that economic growth is good, otherwise, borrowers could not repay their lenders and the lenders would lose their investment.

EQUATION ACROSS BOTTOM OF PAGE:

The negative results of our money system. The combination of the destruction of the commons and the concentration of wealth can only result in social unrest.

LARGE "X" OVER GIFT ECONOMY SYMBOL:

Destruction of the Commons. Abetted by technology, the commodification of formerly non-monetary goods and services has accelerated over the last few centuries, to the point today where very little is left outside the money realm. The imperative of perpetual growth implicit in interest-based money is what drives the relentless conversion of life, world, and spirit into money. Completing the vicious circle, the more of life converted into money, the more people need money to live.

CONCENTRATION OF WEALTH CARTOON:

Economic growth is almost *always* lower than the rate of interest. If debtors cannot make interest payments, they must turn over more and more of their existing wealth to their creditors, leaving wealth in fewer and fewer hands. The rich get richer and the poor get poorer.

Chapter 7: The Crisis of Civilization

The imbalance of debt to existing money in an interest-bearing money system...

...is no longer sustainable.

END OF ROAD

THE RADICAL LEFT

WESTERN ECONOMISTS AND POLITICIANS

Humanity needs an alternative money system.

BALANCE SCALE:

The supply of money and the corresponding volume of debt. Debt has for several decades outstripped the production of goods and services. The continuation of capitalism depends on an infinite supply of new industries, which essentially must convert new realms of social, natural, cultural, and spiritual capital into money. The problem is that these resources are finite, and the closer they come to exhaustion, the more painful their extraction becomes. Therefore, contemporaneous with the financial crisis, humanity has an ecological crisis, as well.

"END OF ROAD" SIGN:

The crisis of civilization. The financial crisis we are facing today arises from the fact that, at some point in the near future, there will be no more social, cultural, natural, and spiritual capital left to convert into money. Centuries of near-continuous money creation has left humanity so destitute that we have nothing left to sell.

This is the process that is culminating in our age. It is almost complete, especially in the United States and the "developed" world. If income from production of goods and services is insufficient to service debt, then creditors seize assets instead. This is what has happened both in the American economy and globally. Eventually, debtors run out of disposable income and seizable assets. The efforts to shore up this edifice cannot work, because it must keep growing — all those debts bear interest. Obviously, the practice of borrowing new money to pay the principal and interest of old debts cannot last very long.

FIGURE ON THE LEFT:

The radical Left. There is no more room for economic growth as the West has known it; that is, no more room for the conversion of life and the world into money. Therefore, even if the more radical policy prescriptions of the Left are followed, hoping by an annulment of debts and a redistribution of income to ignite renewed economic growth, society can only succeed in depleting what remains of our divine bequest of nature, culture, and community.

FIGURE ON THE RIGHT:

Western economists and governments. Most of the proposals for addressing the present economic crisis amount to finding more ways to reignite economic growth—that is, to expand the realm of goods and services. When the financial crisis hit in 2008, the first government response, the bailout of financial institutions, was an attempt to uphold a tower of debt upon debt that far exceeded its economic foundation.

GIFT ECONOMY LOGO:

The alternative to economic growth. The time is here for the reverse process of economic growth to begin in earnest—to remove things from the realm of goods and services and return them to the realm of gifts, reciprocity, self-sufficiency, and community sharing. Note well; this is going to happen anyway in the wake of a currency collapse, as people lose their jobs or become too poor to buy things. People will help each other, and real communities will reemerge. The world of the Gift, echoing primitive gift societies, the web of ecology, and the spiritual teachings of the ages, is nigh upon us.

It tugs on our heartstrings and awakens our generosity. Shall we heed its call, before the remainder of earth's beauty is consumed?

Chapter 8: The Turning of the Age

The "magical" money system is broken while...

...massive attempts to shore it up are failing.

The age is turning...

...as humanity comes of age.

BROKEN MONEY:

The money system imposed on the world. (See Chapters 6 and 7.) When the government's first response to the 2008 crisis—denial—proved futile, the Federal Reserve and Treasury Department tried another sort of perception management. They signaled that the government would not allow major financial institutions to fail. It would have worked if the story these symbolic measures invoked were not already broken. Specifically, what was broken was the story assigning value to mortgage-backed securities and other derivatives based on unpayable loans. Why "magical" money system? Money is nothing more than slips of paper or electronic blips on a computer screen. Those slips of paper and bits are the symbolic representation of an agreement about a story. This story includes who is rich and who is poor, who owns and who owes. Wealth and debts are only as real as the story we agree on that contains them. Unfortunately, or rather fortunately, that story cannot be saved forever. The fundamental reason is that it depends on the maintenance of exponentially growing debt in a finite world. Physically, money is now next to nothing. Socially, it is next to everything; the primary agent for the coordination of human activity and the focusing of collective human intention.

HAND POURING MONEY INTO BANK:

Government attempts to rescue financial institutions. When perception management failed, the next step was to begin injecting massive amounts of cash into failing financial institutions; either in exchange for equity in some financial institutions or in exchange for essentially nothing whatsoever, as in the TARP program (Troubled Assets Relief Program). In the latter, the Treasury Department guaranteed or bought banks' toxic assets in hopes of improving their balance sheets so that they would start lending again, thus keeping the credit bubble expanding. It didn't work. The banks just kept the money (except what they paid to their own executives as bonuses) as a hedge against their exposure to untold quantities of additional bad assets, or they used it to acquire smaller, healthier banks. They weren't about to lend more to consumers who were already maxed out, nor to over-leveraged businesses in the teeth of a recession.

TURNED-UP CORNER OF PAGE:

Humanity's coming-of-age ordeal. The story that is ending in our time, then, goes much deeper than the story of money. It began millennia ago and reached its glorious zenith in the age of the Machine. As the unintended consequences of technology proliferate, we enter the story's final stages, as our communities, our health, and the ecological basis of civilization deteriorate, as we explore new depths of misery, violence and alienation, we enter the story's final stages: crisis, climax, and outcome. Humanity is in the midst of a transition parallel to an adolescent's transition into adulthood. In childhood, the primary aspect of the love relationship is that of receiving. So far, we humans have been children in relationship to earth. In the childhood of agricultural civilization, humanity developed a separate identity. We had our adolescent growth spurt with industry. But also, at this point, a new kind of love relationship emerges; not just one of receiving, but one of giving too. The first mass awakening of the new love consciousness happened in the 1960's with the birth of the environmental movement. As in ancient tribal cultures, having completed the passage to adult-hood, a man or woman takes full possession of his or her gifts and seeks to contribute to the good of all as a full member of the tribe. Humanity is undergoing an analogous ordeal today. With our unique capacities of technology and culture, we will turn to contribute to the good of all.

PART II: THE ECONOMICS OF REUNION

Chapter 9: The Story of Value

What gives money value? Money is not given value by being backed by gold or anything else.

Money has value because of consensual agreement.

  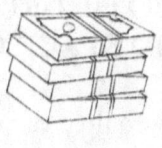

Therefore, humanity can transition to a new consensus – from growth to a gift economy.

Store of value
Unit of account
Medium of exchange

MONEY NEXT TO GOLD COINS WITH LARGE "X":

The theory that money should be backed by something of value. The difference between unbacked and backed currency is not as great as one might suppose. On the face of it, they seem very different: a backed currency derives its value from something real, while an unbacked currency has value only because people agree it does. In reality, this is a false distinction. When the United States announced in August of 1971 that it would no longer redeem dollars for gold within the international banking system, just as it had ceased to do so domestically some four decades earlier, it revealed the gold standard as the convenient fiction that is was.

TWO FIGURES SHAKING HANDS, COMPUTER, AND STACK OF BILLS:

The reality of why money has value. In either case, with backed money or unbacked money, ultimately, what gives money value is the story that surrounds it, a set of social, cultural, and legal agreements. Credit-money (computer- generated and printed bills) is backed by the entirety of an economy's goods and services and, more deeply, by growth. Created as interest-bearing debt, its sustained value depends on the endless expansion of the realm of goods and services. Whatever backs money becomes sacred: accordingly, growth has occupied a sacred status for many centuries. In various guises— progress, harnessing natural forces, conquering final frontiers, mastering nature—we have carried out a holy crusade. But growth is sacred to humanity no longer.

NEW SYMBOL ATOP MONEY MONUMENT:

Money in a sacred economy. Money is inextricably woven into our civilization's defining stories of self, and of humanity, collectively. It is part and parcel of the ideology and mechanics of growth, the "ascent of humanity" to overlordship of the planet; it has also played a central role in the dissolution of our bonds to nature and community. As these stories crumble, and as their monetary dimension crumbles apace, humanity has the chance to consciously imbue money with the attributes of the new stories that will replace them. The sacred economy will bear the following characteristics:

- It will restore the mentality of the gift to our vocations and economic life.

- It will reverse the money-induced homogenization and depersonalization of society.

- It will be an extension of the ecosystem, not a violation of it.

- It will promote local economies and revive community.

- It will encourage initiative and reward entrepreneurship.

- It will be consistent with zero growth, yet foster the continued development of our uniquely human gifts.

- It will promote an equitable distribution of wealth.

- It will promote a new materialism that treats the world as sacred.

- It will be aligned with political egalitarianism and people power and will not induce more centralized control.

- It will restore lost realms of natural, social, cultural, and spiritual capital.

- And most importantly, it is something that we can start creating right now!

Chapter 10: The Law of Return

In an ecology, no species creates waste that other species cannot use...

...except humans. On a practical level, "externalities" (costs of production that someone else pays), must go.

THE THREE CIRCLING ARROWS AND MESSAGE:

The Law of Return. In an ecology (the relations between living organisms and their environments) no species creates waste that other species cannot use — hence the maxim, "Waste is food".

THE EXCEPTION TO THE LAW OF RETURN:

Human activity. Here is a certainty: the linear conversion of resources into waste is unsustainable on a finite planet. More unsustainable still is exponential growth, whether of resource use, money, or population. No other species creates growing amounts of substances that are toxic to the rest of life, such as dioxin, PCBs, and radioactive waste. Our linear, exponential growth economy manifestly violates nature's law of return, the cycling of resources. Would a sacred economy obey the law of return? A sacred economy is an extension of the ecology and obeys all of its rules, among them the law of return. Specifically, that means that every substance produced through industrial processes or other human activities is either used in some other human activity or, ultimately, returned to the ecology in a form, and at a rate, that other beings can process.

FIGURES AT BOTTOM OF PAGE AND SPEECH BALLOONS:

How externalities work. On a very practical level, this vision of sacred economy requires eliminating what economists refer to as "externalities". Externalized costs are costs of production that someone else pays.

For example, one reason vegetables from California's Central Valley are cheaper to buy in Pennsylvania than local produce is that they don't reflect their full cost. Since producers are not liable to pay the current and future costs of aquifer depletion, pesticide poisoning, soil salinization, and other effects of their farming methods, these costs do not contribute to the price of a head of lettuce. Moreover, the cost of trucking produce across the continent is also highly subsidized. The price of a tank of fuel doesn't include the cost of the pollution it generates, nor the cost of the wars fought to secure it, nor the cost of oil spills. Transport costs don't reflect the construction and maintenance of highways. If all these costs were embodied in a head of lettuce, California lettuce would be prohibitively expensive in Pennsylvania. Many industries today can only operate because their costs are externalized. For example, statutory caps on liability for oil spills and nuclear meltdowns make offshore drilling and nuclear power profitable for their operators, even as the net effect on society is negative. Any industry with the potential for catastrophic losses is essentially enacting a transfer of wealth from public to private hands, from the many to the few. It is likewise in the financial industry, where the largest operators can take huge risks knowing that they will be bailed out if those risks fail.

MONUMENT TO A GIFT ECONOMY:

A change is possible. "I keep the income, and someone else pays the costs" reflects the mind-set of the separate self, in which his/her well-being is fundamentally disconnected from the well-being of others. What difference does it make what happens to others? From the perspective of separation, it doesn't make any difference. Profiting by externalizing costs is part and parcel of that perspective. But from the perspective of the connected self, connected to other people and to the earth, other people's well-being becomes paramount because then, everyone benefits. In such a world, the best business decision is the one that enriches everybody—society and the planet. We must create a system that aligns self-interest with the good of all.

Chapter 11: Currencies of the Commons

The Commons belong to everyone...

- Air
- Minerals
- The Planetary Genome
- Centuries-long Accumulation of Human Knowledge, Technology, and Culture
- **THE COMMONS**
- Biota of Local and Global Ecosystems
- The Electromagnetic Spectrum
- Soil
- Water

...therefore, the Commons can, and should be, the basis of our money system...

COMMONS FOR RENT   **NOT**   ~~COMMONS FOR SALE~~

...creating a sacred economy.

~~CONSUMERISM~~   ~~GLOBAL TRADE~~   ~~INEQUALITY~~

| RESPECT FOR MATERIAL GOODS | BUY AND SELL LOCALLY REBUILD COMMUNITY | ENTREPRENEURSHIP CREATIVITY HARD WORK |

LARGE CIRCLE:

The commons. The planet's riches—soil, water, air, minerals, the genome, the biota of local and global ecosystems, the electromagnetic spectrum—were created by no man and should therefore be the property of none, but rather, be held in common stewardship for all beings. The same holds for the accumulation of human knowledge, technology, and culture, which is the bequest of our collective forebears, a source of wealth that no living person deserves less than any other. These truths are closely aligned with the Marxist and anarchist critique of property, but the Marxist solution—collective ownership of the means of production, administered by the state—does not address the real problem. The real problem is that in both the communist and corporate-capitalist systems, a power elite makes and benefits from the decisions of how to deploy society's wealth.

"COMMONS FOR RENT" SIGN VERSUS CROSSED-OUT "COMMONS FOR SALE" SIGN:

The commons should not be owned. Because of today's concentrated private ownership of the commonwealth, the profits that come through mere ownership are highly concentrated. When producers (and ultimately consumers) pay the full cost of embedded energy and raw materials and the fair rental price for the land and other commons, then much of the wealth that concentrates in few hands today will accrue instead to the stewards of the commons. The rental of the commons will benefit all of humanity.

OVERALL MESSAGE:

A new world is possible. Today, access to money, via credit, goes to those who are likely to expand the realm of goods and services. In a sacred economy, it will go to those who contribute to a more beautiful world. There is a near-universal reverence for community, for nature, and for the beautiful products of human culture.

Around these common values, the currency of sacred economy will emerge. What could be a better basis for a money system than those things that are so precious, so sacred, so valuable? Accordingly, part of a sacred money supply will be "backed" by those things of which humans are collective stewards.

THE CROSSED-OUT RESULTS OF TODAY'S ECONOMIC SYSTEM:

How a sacred economy will differ. Respect for material goods will replace consumerism. Buying and selling locally will replace much of global trade while helping to rebuild local communities. Inequality will be greatly reduced while entrepreneurship, creativity, and hard work will all be rewarded.

WHY A NEW WORLDVIEW IS DESPERATELY NEEDED:

The Western worldview of progress is no longer sustainable. Ecological disasters will relentlessly direct our attention to the urgent need to heal the forests, wetlands, oceans, and the atmosphere from the devastation wrought in the industrial era. The urgency of this need will shift our energy away from consumption and war. War is an unavoidable accompaniment to an economic system that demands growth. Whether through the colonization of lands or the subjugation of peoples, the industrialized countries have a constant need to access new sources of social and natural capital to feed the money machine.

Chapter 12: Negative-Interest Economics

Negative interest separates the "store of value" function of money from its function as "a medium of exchange"...

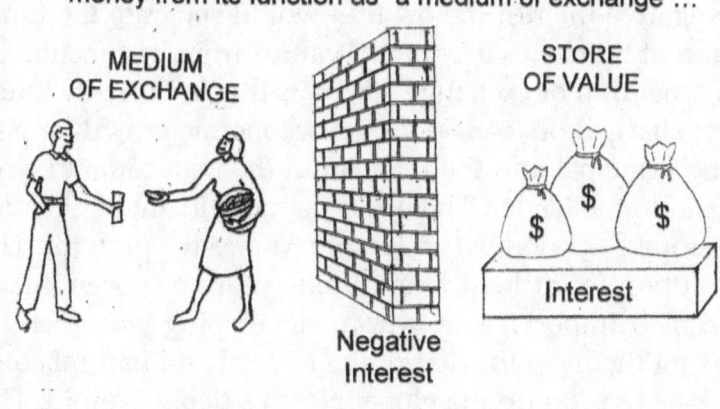

...thereby allowing the "debt bomb" to be defused...

...allowing for the restoration of a gift economy.

BRICK WALL LABELED "NEGATIVE INTEREST" SEPARATES TWO FUNCTIONS OF MONEY:

Negative interest (below 0%) would separate the function of money as a "store of value" from its function as a "medium of exchange". Why is this important? Interest charged on loans demands economic growth or else the principal and the interest on the loan cannot be repaid to the lender. There is little room in any highly developed economy for further domestic growth. The solution for at least twenty-plus years has been, in effect, to import growth from developing countries by using the monetization of their social and natural commons to prop up the global North's debt pyramid. The most common form is debt slavery, where a poor nation is forced to convert from subsistence production and self-sufficiency to commodity production to make payments on foreign loans. Eventually, though, the solution of importing growth must fail too, as developing countries, and the planet as a whole, reach the same limits that developed countries have. Negative interest (sometimes referred to as "free-money") would slow growth since there is no incentive to accumulate and hoard money, keeping it out of circulation. By doing so, it would become a liability as it would incur a carry cost. The physical commons of land, the ecosystem, and the electromagnetic spectrum, as well as the cultural commons of ideas, inventions, music, and stories, must be subject to the same carry costs as money.

BOMB LABELED "DEBT":

The "debt bomb" that nearly brought down the global

economy in 2008. Consisting of high levels of sovereign debt, mortgage debt, credit card debt, student loans, and other debts that can never be repaid, the debt bomb was never defused but just delayed. New loans were issued to enable borrowers to repay old ones, but, of course, unless the borrowers increase their income, which will only happen with economic growth, this only pushes the problem into the future and makes it worse. At some point, default is inevitable. Is there a way out? The answer lies in debt forgiveness and reform of the conventions of money and property. Sooner or later, it will be necessary to face reality—the debts will never be repaid. Either they can be kept in place anyway, and debtor individuals and nations kept in perpetual servitude, or they can be released and the slate wiped clean. The problem with the latter choice is that because savings and the debt are two aspects of a whole, innocent savers and investors would be instantly wiped out, and the entire financial system would collapse. A sudden collapse would result in widespread social unrest, war, revolution, starvation, and so forth. In order to prevent this, an intermediate alternative is to reduce the debt gradually.

What would happen if debt were monetized into free-money? Then, although creditors would not lose their money overnight as they do with defaults or systemic financial collapse, the bailout wouldn't further enrich them either, because they would receive a depreciating asset. As for the debtors, the monetary authority could reduce or annul their debts by any amount it thought appropriate. Yes, the financial interests stand to lose, albeit gradually from this proposal, but what is the alternative? The increasing polarization of wealth is not sustainable.

SYMBOL OF THE GIFT ECONOMY:

What is possible. Amid all the technical details of money and finance, let us not lose sight of the heart of this endeavor: to restore money to its true purpose as a connector of gifts and needs and a means that coordinates human creativity toward a common end.

Chapter 13: Steady-State and De-growth Economics

The end of the growth economy demands a transition to a steady-state economy...

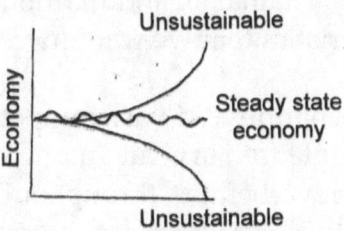

...by shrinking the role of money, yet growing wealth...

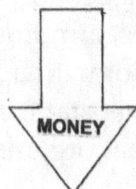
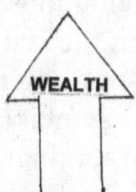

...in part, through disintermediation and the P2P revolution.

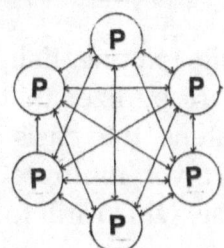

CHART:

Diagram of economy. A core concept of sacred economics is that it is an extension of ecology rather than an exception to it. So we have to ask, is nature fundamentally stable, sustainable, and harmonious? Does it have the characteristics that we want in a society?

The view of nature as a vast competitive arena, a Darwinian struggle for survival among discrete competing organisms, reverberates throughout economic theory. In biology this paradigm has come under increasing challenge, but its economic translation still reigns supreme among most professional economists and policymakers. In the last two decades, a momentous paradigm shift has emerged in biology that emphasizes cooperation, symbiosis, and homeostatic maintenance of wholes larger than the individual organism.

UPWARD CURVE ON CHART:

Infinite exponential growth. Although many people today recognize that continued exponential growth threatens the basis of life on earth, this realization hasn't yet infiltrated into mainstream economic discourse, which still focuses on growth.

DOWNWARD CURVE ON CHART:

Peak and collapse of economy. This is the fear of the pessimists who believe that the exponential curve can only lead to a catastrophic crash back to the baseline. Collapse scenarios involve immense suffering: hundreds of millions or billions of casualties. Moreover, they involve the erasure of the entire edifice of civilization, the good along with the bad.

WAVY LINE:

A steady-state economy. This can occur when there is a peak above sustainable levels followed by a gradual decline toward a steady-state. Phases of rapid growth driven by competition, followed by a phase transition into a steady state, are quite common in nature. Perhaps humanity too is maturing, self-organizing into mutualistic wholes in which competition and growth are no longer primary.

TWO ARROWS:

Less money can mean more wealth. Negative economic growth doesn't entail a decline in wealth at all, nor a decline in the availability of what we call "goods and services". Goods and services at present are defined as *things that are exchanged for money*. If they are provided through some other, nonmonetary, mechanism, then the statistical "economy" can shrink as the real economy — what people make and do for each other — grows richer. This does *not* mean that we must make some sacrifices to our quality of life for the good of the planet. Rather, we need to reduce the role of money.

We don't need to become more altruistic and self-sacrificing, forgoing our own benefit for the good of others. We become richer through the shrinkage of the money realm.

DIAGRAMS AT BOTTOM OF PAGE:

Economic shrinkage that the internet has made possible. *Disintermediation* refers to the elimination of intermediaries: agents, brokers, middlemen, and so forth. The internet can also act as a participatory gift economy as in a P2P (peer to peer) network where there is no consistent distinction between a producer and a consumer and where there is no charge for our "information services".

Chapter 14: The Social Dividend

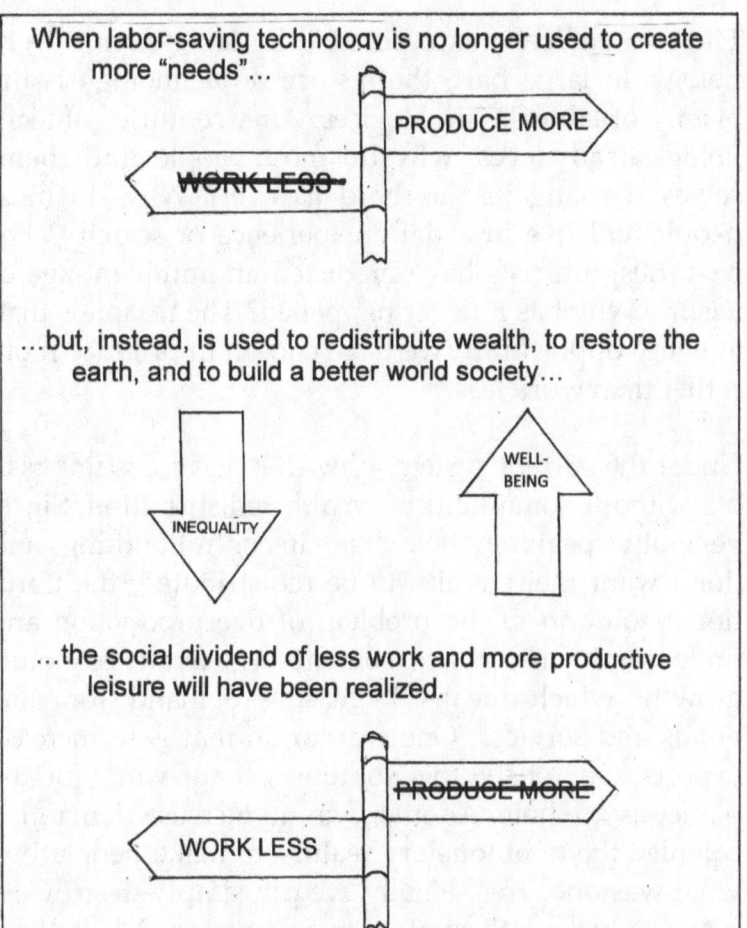

DIRECTIONAL ROAD SIGNS:

The two choices made possible by labor-saving technology. In large part, the history of technology is the history of labor-saving devices. After centuries of technological advances, why do most people find themselves working just as hard as ever? Why do most people still live in a daily experience of scarcity? For centuries, futurists have predicted an imminent age of leisure. Why has it never happened? The reason is that, at every opportunity, we have chosen to produce more rather than work less.

Under the current system, growth in leisure is impossible without some kind of wealth redistribution. Since, generally speaking, the rich are in control of things and don't want their wealth to be redistributed, the traditional solution to the problem of overproduction and underemployment is to somehow generate economic growth, which means increasing demand for new goods and services. One way to do that is to increase exports. Obviously, this solution cannot work for the planet as a whole. Another way to increase demand is colonize the nonmonetary realm—to make people buy what was once free. Finally, we can simply destroy excess production through war and waste. All of these measures keep everyone hard at work when natural demand has been sated.

The ideology of growth says that natural demand can never be sated, that it is infinitely (upwardly) elastic. It assumes an endless supply of new markets, new needs, and new desires. The assumption of limitless needs and therefore limitless demand drives the insanity we see today—and the economic logic that justifies it.

TWO ARROWS:

A reversal of economic dogma is possible. Today, as the natural and cultural commonwealth is exhausted, the context of our choice—work less or consume more—is changing. The age of human ascent is winding to a close, and we must seek to employ the gifts we have developed toward their true purpose in a new relationship to Earth. The age of growth is over. As a society, we have been artificially stimulating demand now for seventy-plus years, through military spending, highway construction, and imperialism. Attempting to uphold economic growth and keep the marginal efficiency of capital ahead of interest, we have trapped ourselves in a pattern of more and more production, whether we need it or not.

Clearly, we possess the means and face the necessity to grow less, to work less, and to turn our energies toward other things. Why hasn't this happened? It ultimately comes down to the depletion of the commons being profitable, and its restoration a matter of altruism. This dynamic must be reversed. Internalization of costs redirects the flow of money and the flow of human activity, away from consumption and toward the sacred. Negative interest money allows investment to go to uses that don't generate even more money than went in and ends the discounting of the future. But more is needed. The question, then, is how to create conditions that allow people to do important work that does not generate an economic return. A social dividend is one answer—enough money for the basics of life. The growth of leisure, or more accurately, the growth of labor done for love, goes hand in hand with the de-growth of the money economy. Humanity is entering its adulthood, a time when physical growth ends and we turn our attention to that which we want to give for the benefit of the earth and our fellow world citizens.

Chapter 15: Local and Complementary Currency

A sacred way of life connects us to the people and places around us, therefore, a sacred economy, must, in large part, be a local economy...

...which presents a catch 22 in that the global economy has virtually eclipsed local economies...

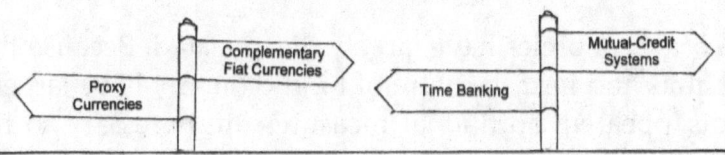

...but there are avenues available to reverse this dilemma.

CLASPED HANDS WITHIN CIRCLE:

Sacred local communities. A sacred way of life connects us to the people and places around us. That means that a sacred economy must be, in large part, a local economy, in which we have multidimensional, personal relationships with the land and people who meet our needs, and whose needs we meet in turn. It is inevitable, when we purchase generic services from distant strangers and standardized products from distant lands, that we feel a loss of connection, an alienation, and a sense that we, like the things we buy, are replaceable. To the extent that what we provide is standard and impersonal, we are replaceable. One of the effects of a homogenous national or global currency is the homogenization of culture. As the money realm expands to include more and more of material and social life, our materials and relationships become standardized commodities, the same everywhere that money can reach.

"LOCAL ECONOMIES" CROSSED OUT:

Local economies have largely disappeared. Because the habits and infrastructure of local economy have largely disappeared, additional measures are necessary to rebuild community-based economies. One of these measures is the localization of money itself. While many things that should be local, such as food, have become global, there are many realms of collective human creativity that by their nature require a global coordination of labor. In general, though, sacred economics will induce the local sourcing of many commodities that are shipped across oceans and continents today. A strong community weaves together social and economic ties. The people we depend on, and who depend on us, are the same people whom we know and who know us. The same goes for the broader community of all beings, the land and its ecosystems. Local economy reverses the millennia-long trend toward the homogenization of culture and connects us to the people and places we see every day. More than fulfilling the longing for community, it also benefits society and the environment. Will local currencies enhance local economies? Most people provide services that only make sense in a vast, often global, coordination of labor. Local currency cannot facilitate a supply and production chain that involves millions of people in thousands of places. Today, local money is not very useful to us because we import nearly everything we use from outside our region.

SIGN POSTS:

Complementary currencies being explored today that may have a role in the coming sacred economy. **Proxy currencies** easily convert to dollars or other national currencies. However, they do little to revitalize local economies or to expand the local money supply. In order for **Complementary Fiat Currencies** to be money, there must be a community agreement that it has value and local sellers of goods and services willing to accept it as such. The effect of fiat currencies is much more potent than that of proxy currencies because fiat currencies have the potential of putting money in the hands of those who would otherwise not have it. **Time banking** is a reciprocity-based work trading system in which hours are the currency. With time banking a person with one skill set can bank and trade hours of work for equal hours of work in another skill set instead of paying or being paid for services. **Mutual-credit systems** include commercial barter rings, credit-clearing cooperatives and local exchange trading systems. When a transaction takes place in a mutual-credit system, the account of the buyer is debited and the account of the seller is credited by the agreed-upon sales price. The development of mutual-credit systems is significant, for credit essentially represents a society's choice of who gets money and how much of it. They replace the traditional function of banks.

Chapter 16: Transition to Gift Economy

The expansion of the money realm has come at the expense of other forms of economic circulation, in particular, gifts.

Thankfully, the money realm is already beginning to shrink, and that degrowth allows new space for gift economics...

...allowing people to meet their needs, whether for goods, services, or money itself, in a great variety of ways.

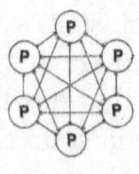 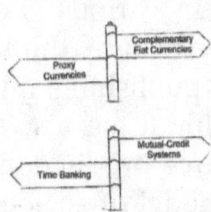 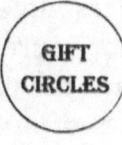

FIGURE EMBRACING MONEY BAG AND CROSSED-OUT GIFT ECONOMY:

The expansion of the money realm. When every economic relationship becomes a paid service, we are left independent of everyone we know, and dependent, via money, on anonymous, distant service providers. That is a primary reason for the decline of community in modern societies, with its attendant alienation, loneliness, and psychological misery. Moreover, money is unsuited to facilitate the circulation and development of the unquantifiable things that truly make life rich.

DEFLATING MONEY SYMBOL AND EMERGING GIFT ECONOMY SYMBOL:

The above scenario is reversing itself. The internet is in important respects a gift network, and it has made it easy to give away information that was once very costly to produce. In various ways, this has pushed services like advertising (think Craigslist) travel agency, journalism, publishing, music, and many more toward the gift realm. It has also facilitated gift-based modes of open-source production. [Open-source production is a new model of socioeconomic production in which physical objects are produced in an open, collaborative and distributed manner and based on open design and open source principles.] What once required paid intermediaries and centralized administrative structures now happen directly. People and businesses are even creating credit, via mutual-credit systems, without the intermediation of banks.

Transition to Gift Economy

Meanwhile, on the local level the ideals of the connected self, the yearning for community, and sheer economic urgency are leading people to restore gift-based community structures. As more and more people recognize the social impoverishment of the conversion of relationship into money, and as the money system itself unravels, people are finding ways to reclaim these functions. One of these is the Gift Circle. In this weekly gathering, participants state one or more things they would like to give and one or more things they would like to receive. Often, it seems, a magical synchronicity of wants and needs unfolds. Could the Gift Circle concept scale up beyond the community level in which people know each other first- or secondhand? In the very long term, we might be able to envision a moneyless gift society based on the model of "circles of circles.

Governments can liberalize tax and banking regulations to give free rein to the new systems of economic circulation emerging today. The commons in which these systems reside, in particular the internet, must be kept public. Governments can also establish and promote mutual-credit systems for business and industry, shielding the domestic or local economy from being preyed upon by international capital.

EXAMPLES OF GIFT ECONOMY SYMBOLS:

Some of the ways people will meet their economic needs. Whether it is for goods, services, or money itself, people will meet them in a variety of ways. Gift circles and online coordination of gifts and needs will allow many needs to be met without money. People will have much more of a sense of being part of a community they can rely on. Complementary, user-created credit systems, along with internet-based P2P (peer-to-peer) lending will make the traditional need for banks unnecessary. On a local level, as well as mediated through global networks, new non-quantified "currencies" of recognition and gratitude will emerge that connect and reward qualitative contributions to society and the planet.

Chapter 17: Summary and Roadmap

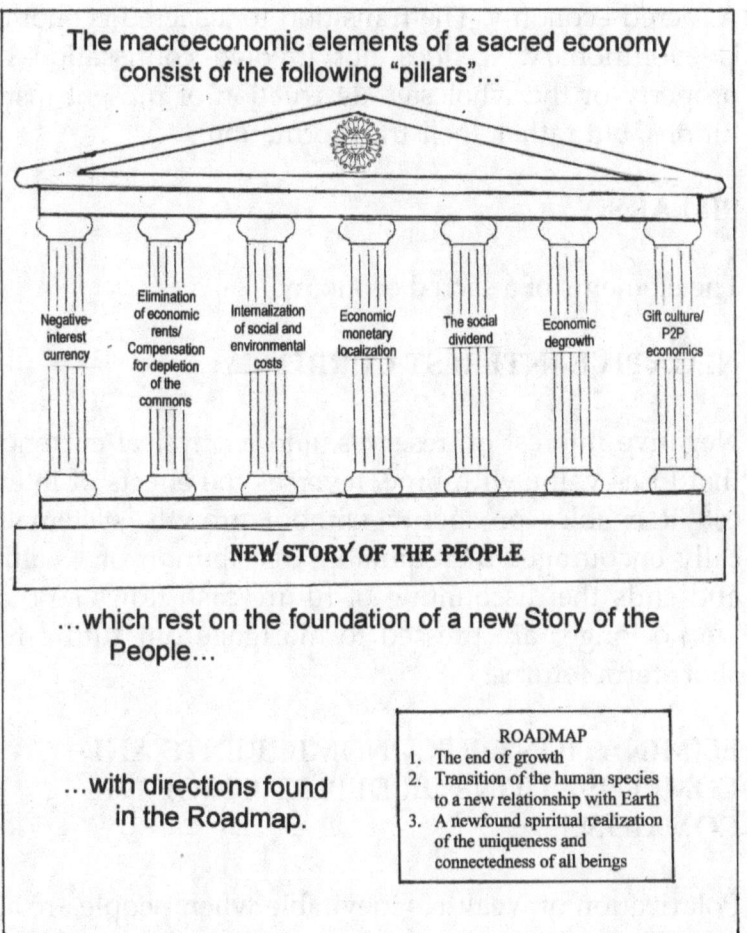

BUILDING:

A sacred economy. The transition to a sacred economy is evolutionary. It does not involve confiscation of property or the wholesale destruction of present institutions, but rather, their transformation.

PILLARS:

The elements of a sacred economy.

NEGATIVE-INTEREST CURRENCY:

Negative interest on reserves, and a physical currency that loses value with time, reverses the effects of interest. It enables prosperity without growth, systematically encourages the equitable distribution of wealth, and ends the discounting of future cash flows so that we no longer are pressed to mortgage our future for short-term returns.

ELIMINATION OF ECONOMIC RENTS AND COMPENSATION FOR DEPLETION OF THE COMMONS:

Polarization of wealth is inevitable when people are allowed to profit from merely owning a thing, without producing anything or contributing to society. These profits, known as economic rents, accrue to the holders of land, the electro-magnetic spectrum, mineral rights, oil reserves, patents, and many other forms of property. Today it is possible to profit by depleting aspects of the commonwealth such as biodiversity, aquifers, soil, ocean fisheries and so on. These properly belong to all of us, and their depletion should only happen by common agreement and for the common good.

INTERNALIZATION OF SOCIAL AND ENVIRONMENTAL COSTS:

It is also possible to deplete the earth's capacity to absorb and process waste, the geosphere's capacity to recycle carbon, and the human body's capacity to deal with toxic pollutants. Today, pollution and other forms of environmental degradation generate costs that are usually borne by society and future generations, not the polluters. Not only is this patently unfair, but it also encourages continued pollution and environmental degradation.

ECONOMIC AND MONETARY LOCALIZATION:

As community has disintegrated around the world, people yearn for a return to local economies where we know personally the people we depend on. Moreover, global commodity production puts localities into competition with each other, fomenting a "race to the bottom" in wages and environmental regulations.

THE SOCIAL DIVIDEND:

Thousands of years of technological advances have made production of the measurable necessities of life extremely easy. These advances, the gift of our ancestors, should be the common property of all humanity. The same is true of the natural wealth of the earth, which was made by no man. The current economic system essentially forces us to work for what is already ours. It is more just to pay out the proceeds of the economic rent compensation, pollution taxes, and so on to all citizens as a social dividend.

ECONOMIC DE-GROWTH:

Over hundreds of years of inventing labor-saving devices, we have at every turn chosen to consume more rather than to work less. This choice, driven by the money system, accompanied an accelerating drawdown of social and natural capital. Today, the option of accelerating consumption is no longer available to us. Absent the driving force of risk-free interest, economic growth will no longer be necessary to promote the flow of capital, and a de-growth economy will become feasible.

GIFT CULTURE AND P2P ECONOMICS:

The expansion of the money realm has come at the expense of other forms of economic circulation, in particular, gifts. That is the primary reason for the decline of community in modern societies.

FOUNDATION MESSAGE AND ROADMAP:

The new Story of the People will see the end of growth, a new relationship with the earth, and a realization of the connectedness of all beings.

PART III: LIVING THE NEW ECONOMY

Chapter 18: Relearning Gift Culture

In our age, there is a distinction between money exchanges and gifts.

Therefore, we must relearn the gift culture which requires a foundation of gift consciousness...

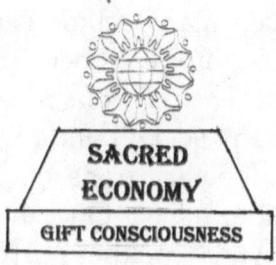

...and the "two-sided coin" of gratitude and obligation.

EQUATION: Money exchanges do not equal gifts. On the personal level, economics is about how to give our gifts and meet our needs. It is about who we are in relation to the world. We have in our age created a distinction between money exchanges and gifts. The former is in the realm of rational self-interest; the latter is at least partially altruistic or selfless. Our goal is to return the spirit of the gift to all aspects of human economy, whether or not money is involved.

FOUNDATION OF SACRED ECONOMY:

Gift consciousness. Consider the ideal of the free gift which many religions embrace. It can be described as having no reciprocity, return, exchange, counter-gift, or debt. The religious ideal of the free gift that doesn't create any social bonds is, ironically enough, very similar to monetary transactions. These also generate no obligation, no tie. Once the money is paid and the goods delivered, neither party owes the other anything. However, gifts are very different. If you give me something, I will feel grateful and desire to give in turn, either to you or to someone else. Either way, an obligation has been created, an assurance of continued economic circulation within the gifting community. Anonymous gifts don't create such ties and don't strengthen communities.

Gratitude, moreover, arises not just from the receiving of gifts, but also from their witnessing. The generosity of others moves us toward generosity ourselves. Gifts don't happen in a vacuum. They expand the circle of self, linking our self-interest with that of someone who, when he has more than he needs, will give us what we need. The resolution of the Age of Separation is a state of universal oneness. We will step into a multidimensional self that identifies with all being, but also with humanity, its own culture, its bioregion, its community, its family, and it ego-self. This was certainly the case in primitive gift cultures. The obligations and commitments that arise from gifts and their expected requital are a glue that holds the society together. We can feel the absence of that glue today.

TWO-SIDED COIN:

Gratitude and obligation. Part of living in the gift is to recognize and abide by the obligation to receive as well as to give. To refuse a gift is to spurn relationship. If gifts create bonds and widen the circle of self, then to refuse to give or receive a gift says, "I refuse to be connected to you. You are an other in my constellation of being." The aversion to obligation enhances the attractiveness of money transactions. When we pay for everything we receive, we remain independent, disconnected, free from obligation, and free from ties. Because it creates gratitude or obligation, to willingly receive a gift is itself a form of generosity. It says, "I am willing to owe you one." By the same token, in refusing gifts we seem to excuse ourselves from the obligations that arise naturally with gratitude.

Clearly then, reluctance to receive is actually reluctance to give. We think that we are being noble, self-sacrificing, or unselfish if we prefer to give rather than to receive. We are being nothing of the sort. The generous person gives and receives with an equally open hand. You can see how pervasive gift refusal is in our culture and how much relearning there is to do. Much of what goes by the name of modesty or humility is actually a refusal of ties, a distancing from others, a refusal to receive. To give and to receive, to owe and to be owed, to depend on others and to be depended on — this is being truly alive.

Chapter 19: Nonaccumulation

Hunter-gatherers lived in a gift culture where possessions were a burden.

However, humanity inherited the farmer's need for security through accumulation which remains the dominant paradigm today...

...but as growth has reached its limit, nonaccumulation is once again possible and desirable.

~~ACCUMULATION~~

FIGURE WITH BALL AND CHAIN:

The role of possessions in hunter-gatherer societies. Wealth is meant to flow rather than to accumulate. This is not a new idea. Wealth only became an accumulation with the rise of agricultural civilization. Because hunter-gatherers are, with very few exceptions, nomadic, possessions are a literal burden to them.

FIGURE WITH HOE NEXT TO BAG OF FOOD:

Farmer and crop. The farmer is sedentary. Moreover, the farmer's livelihood depends on the storage of food, especially in the case of grain-based agriculture. The best security for farmers was to keep large stores of food. From it flowed wealth, status, and many of the habits we identify today as virtues—thrift, sacrifice, saving for a rainy day, good work habits, industriousness, and diligence. We have today inherited and taken to an extreme the attitudes of the farmer, including the agricultural definition of wealth. After agriculture, these attitudes (work ethic, sacrifice of present for future, accumulation, and control) reached their next level of expression in the Age of the Machine which led to undreamed of accumulations of wealth. Today we are in the so-called Information Age, which is yet another intensification of the same attitudes, and which has seen an accumulation of wealth, a contrasting poverty, and an alienation from the natural world far exceeding any precedent.

We are in the transition into a wholly new era, something unknowable and qualitatively different from anything before. We may not know much about it yet, but one thing that is certain about the coning Age of Reunion is that humanity will no longer pretend exemption from nature's laws. Generally speaking, natural systems are characterized by resource flow, not accumulation. The mentality of accumulation is of a similar nature as the ascent of separation, and it is ending in tandem with the Age of Separation as well. Accumulation makes no sense for the expanded self of the gift economy. The integration of hunter-gatherer attitudes into technological society is a completion and not a transcendence of the past.

THE CROSSED-OUT WORD "ACCUMULATION":

Nonaccumulation models hunter-gatherer societies, in which there was great abundance but no accumulation, and in which prestige went to those who gave the most. To give the most, one also had to receive the most, either from nature or from other people. In any event, this kind of prestige is to the benefit of all. It is only when high income translates into accumulation, frivolous consumption, or socially destructive consumption that it makes sense to restrict it. In other words, the problem is not with high income, but rather it is with the results of the income getting stuck at some point in its circulation, accumulating and stagnating. Nonaccumulation is a conscious intention not to accumulate more than a modest amount of assets. It is born not of the desire to be virtuous, but of the understanding that it feels much better to give than to keep, that the seeming security of accumulation is an illusion, and that excessive money and possessions burden our lives. It is deeply aligned with the spirit of the gift, of which a core principle is that the gift must circulate.

Ultimately then, the essence of nonaccumulation lies in the intention with which money is given, lent, invested, or saved. In the spirit of the gift, we focus on the purpose and let the return to ourselves be secondary, an afterthought.

Chapter 20: Right Livelihood and Sacred Investing

Sacred investing seeks to restore the natural and social commons by gifting money – rather than exploiting them for financial gain –...

SACRED INVESTMENT PLAN		TRADITIONAL INVESTMENT PLAN
	**NOT**	
Restoration of commons for beauty		Exploitation of commons for profit

...whether as individuals or through using old accumulations to new purposes...

...and then right livelihood accepts that gift as it does that work.

85

DOCUMENT ON LEFT:

Sacred investment plan. The challenge of excess wealth is to give of it in a way that is beautiful. This is the kind of investment that is aligned with a future economy in which status comes from giving, not having, and security comes not from accumulation, but from being a nexus of flow. It is an entirely different mentality from the traditional paradigm of investment, which we equate with the increase of wealth.

DOCUMENT ON RIGHT:

Traditional investment plan. In a sacred economy, investment has a meaning nearly opposite of what it means today. Today, investing is what people do to preserve their wealth. In a sacred economy, it is what we do to share our wealth. At the most basic level, sacred investing is simply the intentional channeling of this superabundance toward a creative purpose. It begins with the meeting of needs and unfolds into the creation of beauty.

Any "socially conscious investment" scheme that promises a normal rate of return harbors a lie, whether consciously or not. These investments are "robbing Peter to pay Paul" with a commission on the transaction for oneself. The individual who gains from, say, a micro loan to poor African women, is hurting her customers—her fellow villagers. In order to repay the loan, she must charge for the cost of the product plus interest on her loan.

FIGURE HOLDING MONEY:

Individual investor. Interest-generating investments are fundamentally unethical, contributing to the despoliation of the natural and social commons. The same goes for any investment that drives the expansion of the realm of goods and services. As socially conscious investors, you don't want to contribute to the monetization of life and nature.

SKYLINE: Old accumulations. The world sits on top of a huge pile of wealth, the end product of ten thousand years of culture and technology. We have a mighty industrial infrastructure; we have roads and airplanes; we have a vast apparatus already in existence that, for centuries, has been devoted toward the expansion of the human realm and the conquest of the natural world. The time has come to turn the tools of separation, dominance, and control toward the purpose of reunion, the healing of the world. Just as the heirs of fortunes past can turn that wealth to a beautiful purpose, and not worry that the wealth is somehow tainted by its origins, so also do we have the opportunity and responsibility to use the accumulated fruits of our domination of the earth in a beautiful way. In the age of interest—that is, in the age of growth—the primary motivating force behind any new technology was to open up new realms for the conversion of natural or social wealth into money. What will technology look like when devoted to the opposite purpose—the restoration of the planet's health?

HEART-SHAPED CLASPED HANDS:

Symbol of right livelihood. The same principles that apply to right investing apply also to right livelihood. If right investing uses money as gift to support the creation of a more beautiful world, then right livelihood accepts that gift as it does that work. In other words, the key to "right livelihood" is to live off of gifts. What makes it a gift is the motive—that it does not generate even more money in return. Any endeavor that shrinks the money realm draws on gifts.

Chapter 21: Working in the Gift

When we shift into gift mentality, we treat our creations as gifts to other people or to the world. It is contrary to the nature of a gift to specify, in advance, a return gift.

SELLER: I will give you this gift, but only if you pay for it what I think it is worth.

GIVER: I will give you this gift and I trust you to give me what you think is appropriate.

Businesses can work in the gift...

OPEN FOR BUSINESS **AND** **OPEN FOR GIFTING**

...because all professions are sacred.

TWO QUOTATIONS:

Contrast between a seller and a giver. To charge a fee for service, or even for material goods, violates the spirit of the Gift. When we shift into gift mentality, we treat our creations as gifts to other people or the world. It is contrary to the nature of a gift to specify, in advance, a return gift, for then it is no longer giving but rather bartering, selling. A sacred economy recognizes that human beings desire to work; they desire to apply their life energy toward the expression of their gifts. Work is a joy, a cause for gratitude.

The attitude of the seller says, "I will give you this gift — but only if you pay me for it, only if you give me what I think it is worth." The attitude of the giver, in contrast, says, "I will give you this — and I trust you to give me what you think is appropriate." In a sacred economy, compensation will happen through the mechanism of gratitude rather than compulsion.

TWO BUSINESS SIGNS:

Businesses can work in the gift. We are pioneering a new kind of economy, and it is going to take some trial and error to get it right. There are already a number of enterprises today that are implementing gift economies in creative ways. One is the Karma Clinic in Berkeley, California which has been treating people with holistic medicine for two years. Their "bill" states that their consultation was a gift from a previous customer. If they choose, they can "pay forward" for someone else. There are doubtless many more such clinics around the country, and they appear to be quite sustainable. The gift model has also been applied to restaurants where many of them operate on a donation-only basis. Recently the idea entered the mainstream when the national restaurant chain Panera Bread opened a pay-what-you-want store in St. Louis, Missouri. The menu is exactly the same as at its other stores, but the prices are guidelines only. Patrons are asked to pay whatever feels right. The sign at the counter says, "Take what you need, leave your fair share."

On the Internet, of course, an enormous gift economy thrives. Versions of all major types of productivity software are available at no charge. For example, the office suite OpenOffice, a collaborative effort by hundreds of volunteer programmers, is available at no charge. The OpenOffice organization does accept donations and encourages those who have downloaded the software to contribute in various ways. In the meantime, this project has been taken over by the Document Foundation which has further developed the product to become "Libre Office". Lots of bands offer their music for free on the Internet, as well. Astonishingly, there is even a law firm that has incorporated a pay-what-you-will element into its business.

FIGURES:

A variety of professions. The gift model comes especially naturally for professions in which the value delivered is something intangible, such as musicians and artists. This is actually true of every profession since the intangible rides the vehicle of something tangible. Every profession is therefore potentially sacred. Consider the example of farming. What makes food — something tangible — a vehicle for the sacred?

1. It is grown by someone who cares deeply about its nourishing and aesthetic qualities.

2. It is grown in a way that enriches the ecosystem, soil, water, and life in general.

3. Its production and processing contribute to a healthy society.

Sacred food is ensconced in a web of natural and social relationships. It is grown with a love for people and earth that is not an abstract love but a love for this land and these people. We cannot love anonymously. Someone grew sacred food for *me!*

Chapter 22: Community and the Unquantifiable

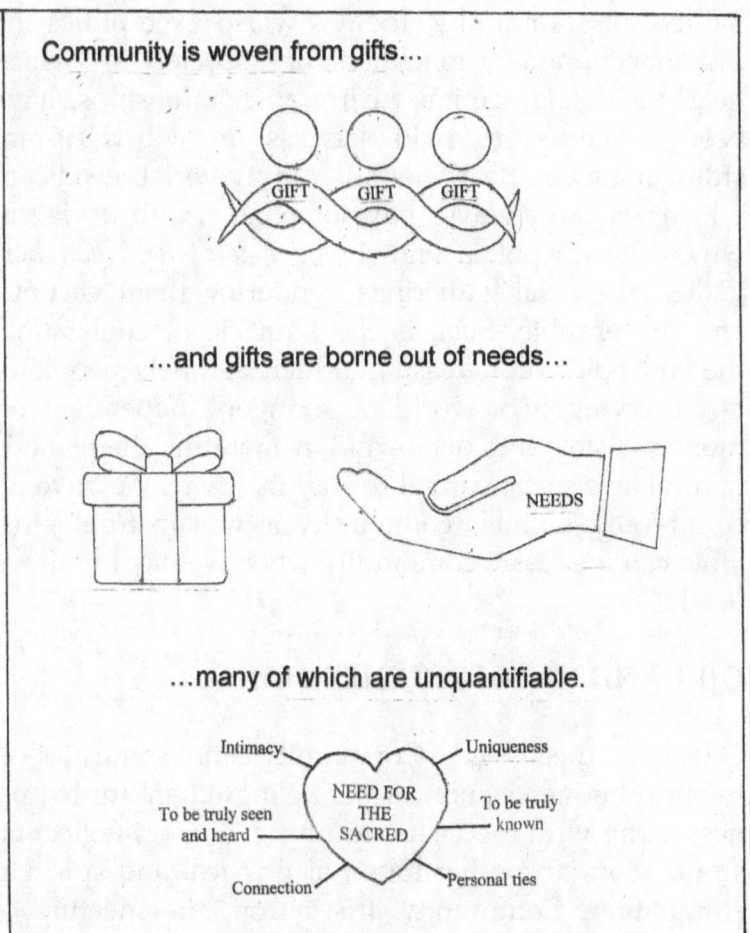

ENTWINED "ARMS":

Symbol of community. Today's world exemplifies the disconnection and loneliness of a society in which nearly all social capital, nearly all relationships, have been converted to paid services; in which distant strangers meet nearly all of our material needs; in which we can always "pay someone else to do it"; in which the unspoken knowledge *I don't need you* pervades our social gatherings, rendering them vacuous and dispensable. Such is the pinnacle of civilization, the end point of increasing affluence: lonely people in boxes, living in a world of strangers, dependent on money, enslaved to debt – and incinerating the planet's natural and social capital to stay that way. We have no community because community is woven from gifts. How can we create community when we pay for all we need?

GIFT AND OUTSTRETCHED HAND:

Gifts must meet needs. Community is not some add-on to our other needs, not a separate ingredient for happiness along with food, shelter, music, touch, intellectual stimulation, and other forms of physical and spiritual stimulation. Community arises from the meeting of these needs. There is no community possible among a group of people who do not need each other. Therefore, any life that seeks to be independent of other people for the meeting of one's needs is a life without community. The gifts that weave community cannot be mere superficialities; they must meet real needs. Only then do they inspire gratitude and create the obligations that bind people together. The difficulty in creating community today is that when people meet all their needs with money, there is nothing left to give. Poor people develop much stronger communities than rich people do. They have more unmet needs.

HEART'S MESSAGE AND ATTACHED WORDS:

Unquantifiable needs. So how do we create community? What will motivate a renaissance in traditional handcrafts, low-tech production, and such? The cessation of hidden subsidies for energy-intensive centralized production and transport will support this renaissance, but will not force it. We will return to local production from a desire to improve life and meet unmet needs – a desire to become richer in the things that really matter. And that will be *our* choice. We can choose to revitalize local, small-scale, labor-intensive production as the only way to meet important human needs. Perhaps there is a hope for community after all, even in the midst of a monetized society. Perhaps it lies in those needs that purchased things cannot satisfy. Perhaps the very things we need the most are absent from the products of mass production, cannot be quantified or commoditized, and are therefore inherently outside the money realm.

Clearly, the transition to a sacred economy accompanies a transition in our psychology. Community, in today's parlance usually means proximity or a mere network, is a much deeper kind of connection than that: it is a sharing of one's being, an expansion of one's self. To be in community is to be in personal, inter-dependent relationship, and it comes with a price: our illusion of independence, our freedom from obligation. You can't have it both ways. If you want community, you must be willing to be obligated, dependent, tied, attached. You will give and receive gifts that you cannot just buy somewhere. You will not be able to easily find another source. You need each other. It is to treat relationship, circulation, and material life itself as sacred. Because they are.

Chapter 23: A New Materialism

Economics is also about the things that humans create.

Today's money-driven economy has sacrificed beauty for efficiency...

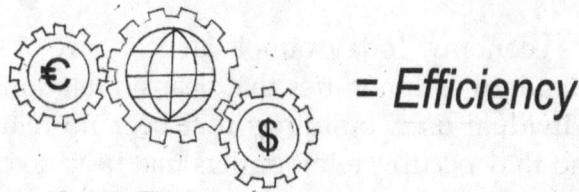

...leaving the world in need of a new materialism.

LIGHT BULB:

Human creativity. Money is the usual subject of "economics" today. On a deeper level, though, economics should be about *things*, specifically about things that human beings create. Compared to the charm and the intense vitality that imbues older objects and structures, ours is a deeply impoverished world. Today, almost everything we use, even if it is expensive, is cheap, reeking of phoniness, indifference, and salesmanship.

SET OF GEARS EQUATION:

Today's economy. Today, ours is an economy of separation: standard commodities that bear no relationship to the individual user, buildings that bear no relation to the land they occupy, retail outlets that bear no connection to local production, and products made in obliviousness to their effects on nature and people. None of these can possibly be beautiful, alive, or whole. By fostering within ourselves a realization of the sacredness inherent in materiality, and by aligning our work with that sacredness, we lay the social and psychic foundation of an economy in which more and more of the things we make and do for each other are beautiful, personal, and alive.

The pursuit of this kind of wealth has not been a public priority for any part of the ideological spectrum for several hundred years. The twentieth-century socialists, for example, rejected any frivolities or indulgences that didn't further measurable material welfare, preferring the utilitarianism of rational efficiency in their grand project of maximizing production to bring plentiful, cheap goods to the masses. Likewise, the progressive activist of today is supposed to shun fine living in pursuit of altruistic ideals. And establishment capitalism is little different: it has re-created and perfected the painfully ugly, utilitarian buildings and objects of socialism. We have created a material world devoid of soul, barren of life and killing of life. All for what? The pursuit of efficiency, the grand project of maximizing the production of commodities, and underneath that, the domination and control of life. This was to be the paradise of technology, life under control, and finally we see it for what it is: the strip mall, the robotic cashier, the endless parking lot, the extermination of the wild, the living, the messy, and the sacred.

WORD "BEAUTY":

The new materialism. The shrinkage of the money realm holds the possibility of liberating more and more of our things from the chains of commodity. After all, we have an overabundance of manufactured goods, the result of standardized mass production and efficiencies of scale. Our tremendous overcapacity indicates that we don't need these efficiencies, nor so much mass production. Trapped by the madness of growth-demanding money, we compulsively produce more and more cheap, ugly things we don't need while suffering a poverty of things that are beautiful, unique, personal, and alive. That poverty, in turn, drives continued consumption, a desperate quest to fill the void left by a material environment bereft of relatedness.

We in rich countries don't even bother repairing most things anymore, as it is usually cheaper to buy new ones. However, much of this cheapness is an illusion coming from the externalization of costs. When we must pay the true price for the depletion of nature's gifts, materials will become more precious to us, and economic logic will reinforce, and not contradict, our heart's desire to treat the world with reverence and, when we receive nature's gifts, to use them well.

SUMMARY OF THE POLITICS OF GOD

HUGH J. SCHONFIELD

I first became aware of Dr. Schonfield's writings in the mid-to-late 1960's. A friend gave me a copy of his book *The Passover Plot*. If you are not familiar with it, its main point is that Jesus planned his own crucifixion with the intent of surviving it, which failed. I liked the book and purchased his follow-up book, *Those Incredible Christians* which details how the Jewish movement that acknowledged Jesus as the expected Jewish Messiah ultimately became the Christian Church. I was deeply appreciative of his "common sense" style of writing, so I was eager to purchase his next book, *The Politics of God*. It was nothing like his other books, but it changed my life. I have come to believe that Dr. Schonfield's vision of world peace and justice through the ministration of a Servant Nation will come to pass.

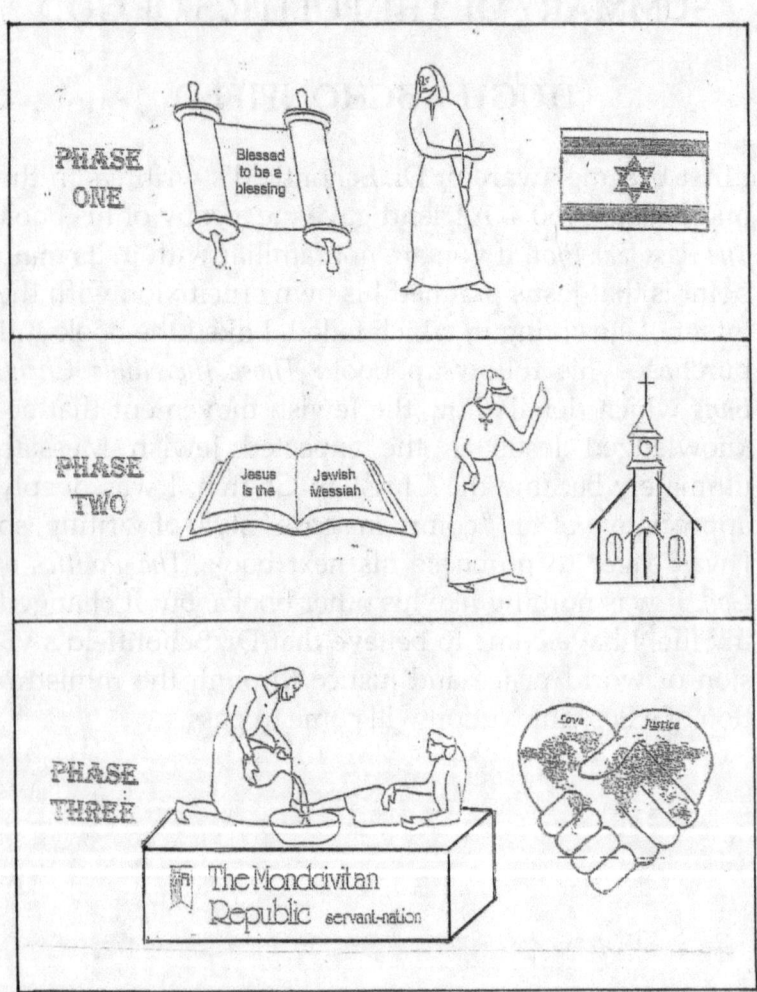

THE POLITICS OF GOD TOP SECTION:

The first phase of the divine plan for bringing justice and peace to the world through the ministration of a Servant Nation.

SCROLL ON LEFT:

The Hebrew tribes who were to become the Jewish people came to believe that their tribal god Yahweh (or simply God with a capital G) had entered into a covenant with them in the Exodus events. He would bless them, and in response, they would be a blessing to the nations. They would be a Servant Nation, exemplifying justice and mercy for all as God had granted them mercy.

FIGURE LOOKING BACK AT THE SCROLL AND POINTING TO THE FLAG ON THE RIGHT:

The Jews never relinquished their belief that they were God's chosen people. However, they did not live up to that expectation as a nation under the David kings. The destruction of the nation was explained by the Hebrew prophets: they had broken God's covenant. When restored to their homeland, their response was to become an exclusive Law Community. The nation was once again destroyed, this time by Rome. The Jews retained their identity as a people and after centuries of undeserved persecution, they established the state of Israel.

MIDDLE SECTION:

The second phase of the divine plan.

BOOK ON LEFT:

Jesus of Nazareth attempted to recall the Jewish people to their divine mission of being a Servant Nation. Although crucified on a Roman cross, his followers declared that he was the expected Jewish Messiah. They expected his imminent return from heaven and the commencement of his earthly reign.

FIGURE WITH HIS BACK TO THE MESSAGE OF JESUS AS JEWISH MESSIAH, POINTING SKYWARD, AND FACING THE CHURCH BUILDING:

Eventually, due to multiple factors, Jesus as Jewish Messiah was transformed from an earthly ruler to God Incarnate. By this time, his mostly Gentile followers believed that his sacrificial death on the cross had atoned for the sins of mankind, granting them an eternity in Heaven. With those changes, the Christian religion was born.

BOTTOM SECTION:

The third, and yet to be fulfilled, phase of the divine plan.

LARGE FOUNDATION BLOCK LABELED "THE MONDCIVITAN REPUBLIC":

The foundation for the contemporary Servant Nation was the culmination of the life work of Hugh Schonfield. Through his guidance and vision, the Mondcivitan Republic was instituted as a legally constituted nation in 1956. While that effort failed, a further development of the Servant Nation must now be realized.

FIGURES ON FOUNDATION BLOCK AND GLOBE ON HEART-SHAPED CLASPED HANDS:

Although Judaism and Christianity are the witnesses to the Messianic vision of a Service Nation, people of good will of any religion or no religion are now called to finally make it a reality.

PART I

In the Prologue to his book Schonfield speaks of a vision he had in 1938: *Suddenly I was in the midst of a stream of lights which poured upon me from every direction, all the colors of the rainbow, so that my surroundings completely disappeared. Inwardly I heard words which came from the Hebrew prophet Zechariah, "Not by might, nor by power, but by my Spirit." At the same time it was conveyed to my mind that what was needed for the deliverance of humanity was a servant-nation. It was the building of this nation to which I was required to address myself.*

Schonfield: *The proposition for which I am arguing is therefore this: first that Godness is at work in our universe, and secondly that this work involves a plan for the accomplishment of which our active cooperation is essential. In so far as this plan affects mankind it is progressively being revealed, so that it may come to have for us a character and intention with which we have identified ourselves as if it were our own, and as if it arose directly from our experience as a race. We are both being wooed and equipped to carry it out, and our time sense is not a factor in determining when fulfillment will take place. Individually and even sectionally we can opt out or retard, though allowance will have been made for this. What man cannot do is to prevent the plan's realization, because in the end we will have been won to bring it to pass. God's will must be done on earth, since of man's own free will it will inevitably become his own will.*

Much of Part One of the book is a survey of Hebrew/Jewish history and how the Jews came to believe that they were God's Chosen People.

Schonfield: *Looking back from the period of the monarchy, the sages of the Israelites saw in the beginnings of the nation the evidence of a singular purpose, which had first been expressed in a Divine call to its progenitor Abraham to leave Mesopotamia and journey to the land of Canaan. There he was told that he would be the ancestor of a great nation through which "all the nations of the earth shall be blessed." Here long ago a novel concept was revealing itself, that of a nation whose greatness would lie in ministry, in the performance of priestly duties for the benefit of mankind. The concept was emphasized in the word of God to Moses on Mount Sinai, "Ye shall be unto me a kingdom of priests, and a holy nation." Israel was distinguished from other nations as a people* **chosen to serve.** *Therefore its very preparation for nationhood entailed the bitter experience of bondage to one of the Great Powers of the ancient world. There could be no harder apprenticeship; but it underlined that the service of God is not as the servitude of men, degrading and humiliating; it is manifested in disinterested* [impartial] *love. Specifically it was laid down in the laws of Israel, "Thou shall not oppress a foreigner: for ye know the heart of a foreigner, seeing ye were foreigners in the land of Egypt" and again, "The foreigner that dwelleth with you shall be unto you as one born among you, and thou shalt love him as thyself; for ye were foreigners in the land of Egypt."*

Of course the reality of Israel's history did not match the vision set before them, either as a nation under the David kings, or as the chastised Law community established upon their return from exile under Cyrus of Persia.

Schonfield: *But one of the things which did come in with the Persians was the idea of a Cosmic Drama, an age to age contest between Light and Darkness, Good and Evil, which in the end would be crowned by the victory of Righteousness. This was to give rise to a developed Jewish eschatology, in which this idea was brought into relationship with the teaching of the Prophets with emphasis on a coming Day of the Lord and the appearance of Messianic personalities.*

How could the Jews be stirred to spiritual action among the nations? We find the issue affected by two major circumstances. First, the victories of Alexander the Great brought East and West together within the framework of a united world concept. The Jews were brought in closer contact with Greek culture, and became much more widely distributed by increasing settlement in other lands. Second, the attempt by one of the heirs to part of Alexander's empire, the Syrian king Antiochus Epiphanes, to compel the Jews to adopt the Greek religion made them take their faith and its universal implications much more seriously. Both the wider contacts and the revivalist fervor caused the Jews to engage in missionary work as never before. The intensity of effort was closely linked with a reading of the Signs of the Times, which now insisted that the Last Days were at hand. As a result the knowledge of God and of a distinction between Jews and all other nations became widespread. But the Jewish impact was made very little in a spirit of love and service, as their propaganda literature indicates, and therefore was still far removed from the objects of a servant nation.

This was the world which Jesus as Messiah encountered.

Schonfield: *As it was, Jesus as Jewish Messiah set the seal on those aspects of Jewish faith which insisted that the love of God was to be made manifest in the treatment of all persons as beloved of God. No one was to be regarded as objectionable on grounds that he was an alien, a sinner, a heathen. Neither in any circumstances was anyone to be treated with hostility. No people of God could function which lorded it over others. It could never be a curse to those whom it was designed to bless.*

The concept of the Jewish Messiah was that the Messiah was to be in relation to Israel as Israel was to be in relation to the world.

Schonfield: *A new recruit to the Messianist cause, the Hellenic Jew, Saul of Tarsus, threw himself ardently into an all out effort to gain converts opportunity to join the ranks of Israel by faith in the Messiah...The new Israelites, who had been former pagan Gentiles, colored their faith with Gentile notions and created the religion of Christianity in which Jesus was worshipped as God incarnate instead of being followed as Messiah...The People of God was effectively rent in two, with the new religion persecuting and vilifying the old. But the Jews did not perish. While Christianity became more other-worldly they [the Jews] remained as a living reminder of a purer faith, which also insisted on the earthly fulfillment of the ancient vision of a Messianic age of world peace and justice....Christianity became the official religion of the Roman Empire, and as such it was able to promote powerfully a widespread acknowledgement of God and a relinquishment by many nations of a cruder idolatry to an extent that the Jews had been incapable of achieving. As a result a very important halfway step was being taken towards the ideal, and Jewish ethical teaching through Christianity was accepted as* *the standard of conduct by which society, individuals and kingdoms should be guided.*

Peoples, however, were being Christianized on the whole superficially. The objective of the Church was not to call out of the nations a ministering servant-nation, but to bring as many peoples as possible under its sway. It was in fact aiming at a new Romanism, the concept of a Holy Roman Empire.

We have for some time now passed beyond Biblical history, and have to note that later developments were not less significant. What in particular we have to observe, in spite of a number of setbacks, is a progressive resistance to Romanism, the doctrine of a self-appointed Common Superior, and the growth of a universalistic humanitarianism. [Note: Elsewhere Schonfield defines Romanism as "claiming the right to dominate by reason of asserted superiority or from motives of self-interest."]

The foundations for democracy were laid in the town marketplaces and the rise of nation-states created the groundwork for international law. The Age of Reason with its gospel of Liberty, Equality and Fraternity dawned. More and more people were being included as active participants in social and political life. A sense of social responsibility developed which encouraged anti-slavery legislation, emancipation of negroes and Jews, the trade unions, the care of the aged and destitute, the more humane treatment of criminals and the insane. However, this extension of consciousness did not spell the end of Romanism. In Capitalism and Communism it produced additional varieties of imperialism.

Schonfield: *The reading of events which we have furnished has emphasized two contrasting principles, those of domination and service, the one tending to slavery and the other to liberation...At our present stage of development we should now be able to detect that what we have termed Romanism is a wrong employment of Godness qualities, and Messianism a right one. If we choose Romanism, even for what appear to be good ends, what we construct and aim at will not work out. If we choose Messianism, which may seem to be weak and ineffective, the result will none the less be beneficial. We have, therefore, standards by which we can test the validity of any course of action. If it calls for force or domination, sooner or later it will fail. If it calls for love and service, even if it involves temporary suffering, it will succeed...*

The time is ripe for a further expression of Messianism in keeping with past indications to manifest itself to meet our desperate need. We can profit by it or reject it for our generation, either totally or partially, and our decision will govern what we have to endure. But if we fail it will crop up again and again, if need be, for ages unborn. In the end the Divine Plan will be our plan.

PART II

Part One of Schonfield's book flowed along smoothly as a historical narrative. However, Part Two is more topical, so I will treat each chapter separately.

Chapter 1: Twentieth Century Man

Schonfield: *This century of such vast promise and performance, hailed as that of the Common Man, has proved to be one of increasing doubt and uncertainty, frustration and sense of impotence, and worst of all the century of the Great Fear.*

He explains what won't work: centralized governmental control is too big and impersonal and, therefore, Romanism must be employed for its success. Schonfield addresses the attempts of small groups of well-intentioned people to make practice square more nearly with the principles they espouse. While commendable, the people involved cooperate and care for each other because they are already unified.

Therefore, **Schonfield asks**: *"Can there be found a comprehensive ideology to unite mankind, which permits and welcomes diversity within the kinship, and does not have to act coercively?"... There are plenty who offer panaceas for the various world problems; but this is not what is required, since there is no universal will to accept them or try them out. The only possibility for the success of any of these propositions is that they should first pass the test of a sufficiently* *organized society within society which agrees to conduct the experiment.*

As we will see, this is the option that Schonfield chose in building a Servant Nation. It will accomplish what the Jews as the state of Israel and the Christian Church as a religion have rejected and therefore can never accomplish.

Chapter 2: War and Law

There has been a proliferation of sovereign states in the twentieth century.

Schonfield: *This has conferred on many more peoples the capacity of self-expression and permitted them to have a say in world affairs. But it has also demanded a more universalistic approach to the problems of world order, since without it a high percentage of the new states could have no possibility of survival either politically or economically. Their existence also added to the risks of minor wars being blown up into large scale wars, and even global wars... Never previously has it [war] constituted a threat to all humanity... There has therefore had to be a movement on the part of states toward regulating their relationships. Unfortunately, nationalistic and ideological interests have been so prominent, and governmental cunning so much in evidence, that organization for peace has continually been handicapped.*

However, there were also positive aspects. The Geneva Conventions of 1864 established the International Red Cross which created a category of non-combatants to minister to the wounded. The establishment of this agency was a remarkable humanitarian achievement, by which states for the first time accorded recognition to a category of neutralized persons. The Hague Conferences of 1899 and 1907, in an attempt to reduce the possibility of war, promoted the use of one or more friendly powers as mediators in any international dispute. Here again there was recognition of a special role, this time to be played by states.

However, these enlightened innovations could not prevent two major wars in the first half of the twentieth century. In the aftermath of the First World War, President Wilson of the United States declared that if there was to be world peace, nations must be governed by law. He was instrumental in establishing the League of Nations which proved to be ineffective in that role. The United Nations, created after World War Two, was no more effective in achieving world peace. In fact, it chose to take the military action of defending South Korea.

Schonfield: *Peace secured by violence is not peace... There is therefore no short-cut to the solution of the problem of war, unsatisfying as this admission must be to those who realize the gravity of our present perils, and want to do something urgent and decisive to remove them. We are forced to tackle initially the causes of war, not one major cause, but all the causes; and this will demand of us not only intelligence and a judicial detachment, but a total commitment to a higher law of love which sublimates violence.*

What object can man choose as a genuine value to enable him to achieve control over his destructive militant propensities? I believe it to be one for which man is qualified more than any other creature, that of mutual disinterested [impartial] *service...Service is the only quality which can make authority endurable and endure. It puts into action what Paul in a famous passage said of love...The obvious conclusion is that love and friendship should embrace all humanity, that we should love all our brothers indiscriminately.*

Chapter 3: One World

The chief incentive for world unity has been the urgent need to devise a practical method to assure perpetual peace. The principal proposals for world unity envision some form of World Federation, because this permits the continued existence of sovereign states.

Schonfield: *A United States of the World is totally unpracticable while ideological conflict exists. The principal ideologies are poles apart in their thinking about the character and structure of society, and consequently about the manner in which world government should function...Facing realities, the life of man socially and politically, has been too compartmentalized for him to be capable as yet of adequate comprehensive of the larger unity required of him...From an impersonal viewpoint the world becomes much smaller, but from the viewpoint of the average individual it has become infinitely larger...The more you try to draw him on into that wider association, the more he will resist and pull back. He will assert his right to independence, to live his own life, which means to stay in the little world which he can just about cope with, and in which he feels comfortable.*

In spite of the problems associated with world federalism, there are many who believe in the concept of world citizenship. They reflect the recognition that the world is a unity and that there is a need for a higher allegiance to all humanity without distinction or discrimination. Many thoughtful individuals and groups have been stressing the cultivation of a world outlook and an education for world citizenship by teaching the history of man in his cultural, social and political development along-side national history. They have been devising world auxiliary languages and have been fostering in many connections closer international relations and the setting up of world institutions.

Schonfield: *All such activities have been creating important precedents or in some way laying foundations for the future...It has remained, however, to bring world citizenship to birth in a manner which would enable it to be recognized and acknowledged as a real status available to those who are spiritually ready for it. A new category of human beings has to appear, representative of a prior and overriding right of loyalty to mankind. Without this, since states and peoples are still a long way from preparedness for a development which would embrace them all, there can be no substantive advance towards world unity. Thus a factor in world affairs has to manifest itself, which has not been entertained by people in general and has not entered into the careful calculations of statesmen, one which makes world citizenship visible and tangible.*

Chapter 4: The Brink or the Eve?

Is humanity on the brink of disaster or on the eve of a tremendous beneficial change?

Schonfield: *The modern inheritors of the Jewish-Christian tradition, brought up on the Bible and nurtured in its imagery and expectations, have correspondingly sensed the purport of the signs of their own times. The former age was initiated by the seductions of Hellenism, which were countered by Messianic Judaism with its proliferation of eclectic sects and an explosion of missionary zeal. In the same way the new eschatological period was heralded by the Age of Reason, which evoked the Christian response of like sects and missionary activity. The evangelical revival strongly emphasized the Second Advent of Christ and encouraged the fresh interpretation of the prophetic records in relation to the contemporary scene. Again there was a busy engagement in calculating the dates of the Last Times.*

If a Divine Plan for mankind was in progress in biblical times it must be continuing to operate. And since we are living in another crucial period for humanity, much more dangerous and complex than the beginning of the Christian era, the appropriate expression of Messianism for our time must manifest itself. The nature of it will necessarily be in line with the tenor of the previous indications, but representing a new expansion and a more sophisticated development... There will be a second coming of Christ, but not as anciently depicted, just as the circumstances of the previous advent were not at all as many students of prophecy had anticipated. What we should expect is that through better knowledge an understanding of the real Jesus and his Messianic message will be given back to us, thus restoring him to us as he has not been seen for nearly two thousand years, so that the right actions can follow.

It is plainly intimated that what is in travail to be born is the first whole-world age, the first era in which man can become united, the first actual achievement of world citizenship. This could not have begun to happen before the developments of the past two centuries and more. We were only starting to be emancipated. We had not sufficiently explored our planet geographically and recovered enough of our world's history. We had not the means of speedy travel and communication. We did not possess the knowledge, equipment and resources to bring the whole earth into occupation and productivity, and make food, goods and services universally available. We could not adequately educate people and improve physical and social conditions. We were not compelled by mass-destructive weapons and the exigencies of the conquest of Space to organize for global integration...On the basis of a Divine Plan a further manifestation of Messianism **has** *to appear in a manner appropriate to our time, but arising from the previous expressions of it. We are not on the brink of doom, but on the eve of regeneration.*

Chapter 5: A Time of Testing

Schonfield: *When the seers of two thousand years ago proclaimed the impending Messianic judgment they described it as a Time of Testing which is coming upon all the world. We ourselves are now in such a time. Former convictions, values and beliefs are in the melting pot. In almost every connection they are being challenged and tested to determine their worth and validity. There is a growing unwillingness to take anything for granted, and things once regarded as fixed and settled are now being ruthlessly scrutinized and frequently rejected. Those who are sentient, whether intelligently or instinctively, realize that we have to adjust to very great* *changes, and therefore we have to free ourselves from hidebound positions and examine every proposition afresh. There is nothing that is now sacred and immune.*

Giving examples from the former Messianic period, Schonfield concedes that the present experience will not be a pleasant one.

Schonfield: *It is never easy to distinguish between healthy and unhealthy criticism; and those who believe themselves to be in the right usually find it most difficult to acknowledge that they could be wrong... There are two sides to every question, and it takes a deal of grace when one is passionately committed to one side to see the virtues of the other side. Especially is this so when the clash is between an order which is passing away and another which is coming to birth. The tendency is to take extremist positions, with all that these entail of venom, hostility and recrimination.*

We cannot yet know what form world unity will ultimately take; but we can look so far ahead as a co-operating association of nations, not dominated by any Herrenvolk, but guided by a conscience-nation, as free, interpenetrative, and lacking in location as the soul is in the body...In seeking our salvation we have perhaps been looking in the wrong place, the abodes of politicians and prelates. With our power mindedness we have gone automatically to these quarters...But there is hopeful evidence, as we have seen, in the progressive growth of a world-minded minority which has surmounted the limiting factors of race, creed and territory. This minority, which has recreated the Elect Remnant, bears all the marks of ability to make the world conscience articulate and effective.

It is the Divine Plan that there should be such a nation, introducing a quite unexpected factor into world affairs at this juncture, the People of Man and the People of Tomorrow, in which at first on a small scale those who are called out of all races and climes, peoples, tongues and nations, will mingle their blood and manifest a common love of humanity. The vision has had a long history of partial fulfillment, but the time has now come when full realization begins to be practicable.

Chapter 6: The Third Phase

Schonfield: *It has been the affirmation of this book that Messianism is the expression of the Politics of God...But the Jews and Christians, by their waywardness, broke the compact, and as a consequence the Plan, which demanded effective human cooperation, was prevented from coming to fruition...The failure in turn of Jewish and Christian Israel now appears providential in the light of history, since mankind's perilous situation has become so much graver that a further unfolding of the character of the Divine Plan in a fresh phase of expression is imperative...But they* [Jews and Christians] *have also been preserved as the Two Witnesses, whose testimony offers convincing evidence of the Divine Plan and what it has portended.*

Where the religions have failed is in offering ivory-tower security, an inducement to get away from the hurly-burly of involvement or to endure with piously folded hands. We are not in this world to prepare for the next. We are in this world to make it better...Thus a Third Phase in the unfolding of the Divine Plan has had to become manifest... The Servant-Nation is being reconstituted from the sentient minority which is ready and willing to undertake the responsibilities of world citizenship for the sake of all humanity. Jews and Christians should be the first to sign on for service. But this time the door is open to people of all religions and of none, who hear the call and are prepared to accept the principles by which the new nation is governed and the conditions of its citizenship.

The Christian dilemma is that while Christians believe they are adherents of a religion they cannot get away from Romanism, and have to act correspondingly inside states which have quite other aims and methods than the Messianic...God's nation is not a Power dominating and controlling the nations, but a nation among the nations, serving them and setting them a national example. It is what I have called a Christ-Nation...The Christ-Nation, the Servant-Nation, is not going to work any miracles. Its work will be slow and arduous, and very largely unspectacular, quite unattractive and unconvincing to those in a hurry, who will continue to busy themselves as of yore with the speciously authoritative.

The existence of the Servant-Nation does not give rise to a problem of duel allegiance, for the allegiances are not equal. There is a primary allegiance to mankind, and a secondary allegiance to the state. These allegiances should not be imagined to be opposed, since the good of the whole benefits every part.

And what will the Servant-Nation do?

Schonfield: *We can employ an agency that is not a state,* yet sufficiently statelike, to experiment in world unity and fresh forms of social and political life. In this way inevitable progress will be robbed of its terrors, since it will first be tested out on the harmless proving-ground of the Servant-Nation. But the Servant-Nation has many other valuable and essentials functions to perform. During the world wars there was need for neutrals as intermediaries...With the Servant-Nation we will have a world agency equally serving all peoples, with no axe to grind and no territory to defend, which cannot take sides in any dispute, and which, therefore can be an acceptable mediator...Standing for a peaceful united world community its aim will be to set a living example of nationhood at its best, to investigate and experiment with policies making for closer cooperation and integration, until it can appear by common consent what form pf planetary society is most suitable, not as a power-structure, but on a basis of mutual fellowship. Through its universality of distribution the Servant-Nation in this respect can be used creatively in the character of an experimental working-model.*

Chapter 7: Plan in Progress

Schonfield: *The annunciation concerning the Servant-Nation took place on Monday the 26th September 1938 [in London]. From a human angle the coming of a People of Peace could not have been heralded at a less propitious moment. With Hitler's insatiable demands, at the time on Czechoslovakia, no one knew what a day would bring forth. The world was on the brink of another world war, and the Munich pact would bring only a brief uneasy respite...After years of suffering and destruction the immediate danger was overcome; but the spirit behind it had not been eradicated,* *only temporarily subdued. But the Servant-Nation in its new expression had yet to be born, and then to experience all the pains and difficulties and disciplines of growing up. It has taken thirty years for it to reach maturity, so that it would be ready and equipped for its mission.*

The Constituent Assembly of the Servant-Nation, the Mondcivitan Republic (formerly known as the Commonwealth of World Citizens), was held in August 1956.

Schonfield: *Prior to the Assembly a copy of the Constitution had been transmitted to the Secretary-General of the United Nations and to all Governments, and at the close of the proceedings a Council was elected to prepare the way for the first experimental Parliament...The formation of a Government was important because it facilitated communication with the state governments. Mondcivitan ministers could correspond with their opposite numbers in the different countries according to protocol and receive replies appropriately.*

Helpful initiatives were taken during the life of the first Parliament to promote world peace and international understanding, both directly and by preparing resolutions for sponsorship by states in the General Assembly of the United Nations...The following year the Mondcivitan Republic intervened over the Cuban Crisis. As President I communicated personally with President Kennedy and Chairman Kruschchev on October 25th...How influential this letter proved cannot for certain be known; but I am now making it public because of what transpired, and it is the fact that Mr. Kruschchev in his concluding letter to President Kennedy on October 28th substantially echoed my words and thoughts.

Schonfield wrote his book *the Politics of God* in 1970. Today the Mondcivitan Republic is little more than a memory. (It does have a Facebook page maintained by Stephen A. and Sandra Engelking.) However, Schonfield was convinced that the Divine Plan could not be thwarted by mankind; if his generation were to reject it, a future generation would embrace it and bring it to fruition. The time is short. Has that generation and their moment arrived?

About the Mondcivitan Movement

REBUILDING A *HOLYSTIC*[3] SERVANT NATION OF MANKIND

Mondcivitania is a virtual servant nation composed of all those who are willing to try and live by its principles which are based on love for our fellow human beings.

Being a holy nation has nothing to do with church membership or religious affiliation, nor with personal salvation and an afterlife. Our bond is the shared realization that all of life on this planet is a unity and that we are meant to live in love and community with everyone. We are by no means perfect, or can ever hope to be, but by following the Principles below, we can serve as an example to the rest of humanity that a beautiful world is possible. We don't need the rule of law which always protects the elite sector, but rather, the law of love which gives meaning and purpose to everyone. As we are a people, there is no formal membership—you are already a Mondcivitan if you find it right to live by these principles:

1. No-one is an Enemy

The Mondcivitan Republic acknowledges none as en-

---

3   With the spelling "holystic" the intention is to emphasize the idea of a "holy" Servant Nation (in other words—set apart for a special purpose, to be an exemplary people qualified to mediate on the behalf of mankind). It also includes the idea of holistic—the whole is greater than the sum of the parts.

emies, no matter what they may do; for to admit the existence of an enemy is to create a barrier, darkening understanding, breeding hatred, and giving encouragement and licence to cruelty and inhumanity.

2. No-one is a Foreigner

The Mondcivitan Republic recognizes none as foreigners, or of a lower dignity, since all belong to the same human race. There shall be identical treatment of those outside the Commonwealth as of those within it, treatment that is founded on reverence for the human personality.

3. Service to All

The Mondcivitan Republic shall ever promote and actively assist measures for the welfare and equitable unification of mankind, and shall at all times respond to the extent of its ability to calls for aid in emergency or catastrophe.

4. Complete Impartiality

Neither the Commonwealth, nor any of its citizens, shall under any circumstances engage in war or in preparation for war, or in aggression, oppression, or wilful misrepresentation. The Mondcivitan Republic shall ever hold itself free from all alliances, agreements and contractual obligations, whether open or secret, which can have the effect of favoring any group, party, section, or state, or any interests whatever, to the hurt or detriment of any others.

5. Work for Peace

The Mondcivitan Republic shall study to be impartial in all its relations and judgments, and shall labour in the cause of mediation and reconciliation.

6. True Democracy

The character of the Commonwealth is democratic and cooperative, based on mutual service and respect, holding all people in honor in public and private.

7. Equity and Justice

In its government and internal economy the Mondcivitan Republic shall continually seek to cultivate and display those standards of conduct which are equitable and just.

We do have a choice however and we can start to try to live by these principles in our personal lives. It is time for all those who ascribe to them to stand up and be counted as a citizen of this people in service to mankind. So all your comments and reports of activities to further these principles are welcome.

Mondcivitania is the successor to the Mondcivitan Republic (Commonwealth of World Citizens) legally constituted in 1956 and the International Arbitration League founded by Nobel Peace Prize Winner (1903) Sir William Randal Cremer.

Please join us at

www.mondcivitan.org

https://www.facebook.com/groups/mondcivitania

More information is also available at:

https://en.wikipedia.org/wiki/Mondcivitan_Republic

http://www.schonfield.org/

www.ingramcontent.com/pod-product-compliance
Lightning Source LLC
LaVergne TN
LVHW032005070526
838202LV00058B/6310